The *Kingdom ~Building* Church

EXPERIENCING THE EXPLOSIVE POTENTIAL OF
THE CHURCH IN KINGDOM~BUILDING MODE

Ben R. Peters

Published by
Kingdom Sending Center
P. O. Box 25
Genoa, IL 60135

www.kingdomsendingcenter.org
ben.peters@kingdomsendingcenter.org

ISBN 13: 978-1514893999

Cover and book design by *www.ChristianBookDesign.com*

Contents

Preface

This book is not written as a critique of the modern church, although the current state of the church can use a lot of improvement. Rather, the purpose of this book is to discover what the heart of God cries out for, and what the plans of God are for His church in this great season of harvest. And believe me, He has incredibly great plans for us, His body, on this earth before He returns in all of His glory and majesty. He is the King of kings and we will be preparing His royal palace and expanding His borders with great enthusiasm and effectiveness.

What God is shifting is the way we look at church, both the universal and what we call the local church. I believe He is shifting our paradigms by using both the top-down and the bottom-up methods. That is, church leaders will get excited about God's vision for the church and will teach it to their people. At the same time the people will be getting the same revelation on the grass-roots level and will be encouraging their leaders to lead them in a new direction.

So what is that new direction? How will church life change? How will our personal lives change? What are the rewards for pursuing a new direction? These are some of the questions that this book will address as we explore this subject. Expect some radical challenges to the status quo. Expect some surprises! Keep your heart open. Adopt a reformation/restoration heart attitude. God has a better way of "doing church" than we have experienced to date in our generation. His eyes are searching throughout the whole earth, seeking for those whose hearts are in rhythm with His heart and whose thoughts are in harmony with the mind of Christ. If He wants to reform and restore His church, than I want the same thing. If He is contented with a weak, divided and compromising church, then I will be content with that as well. But I am totally convinced that He is not content with the status quo and neither am I. Let's join together to pray His prayers – especially the prayer of Jesus in John 17. That's a great place to start! Then let's watch and see what God can do when we allow Him to put us in Kingdom-building mode.

Chapter 1

What Really Are We Seeking?

Before we get into the meat of this chapter, I want to make one thing perfectly clear, no matter what information will follow this declaration. God is not an angry God towards His truly blood-bought children, the church of Jesus Christ. He loves the church, even when it doesn't have much of a clue what He is desiring from her.

God has tolerated, I'm sure with a measure of sadness, some very bad behavior from many of His leaders of the past. For example, Martin Luther, who was so powerfully used to restore the doctrine of justification by faith, totally missed it with regard to God's heart toward the Jews. He made some terrible statements about them, as did other earlier and more recent church leaders. The persecution which resulted from their bad theology still makes it difficult for many Jews to accept Jesus as their Messiah.

But God has always been full of mercy and longsuffering with His people, as David clearly repeated over and over again in the Book of the Psalms. We, His children, need to have the same patience and a heart of forgiveness towards those who don't seem to get it today. For more than likely, tomorrow, God will show us that we didn't really get it either. We may have had some great revelation, but God never gave it all to one person or to one denomination. He always intended that as the body of Christ, we should be interdependent on one another, rather than independent from one another.

Meanwhile, like the patient Father that He is, He realizes that we are just children, not fully grown up and not really aware how immature we are or lacking in wisdom. He does use a little direction correction and discipline when it's needed, but He never rejects the children that He has made His own.

With that hopefully clear disclaimer, let's proceed with the subject of this chapter: What are we seeking?

THE CALL TO MINISTRY

When most young Christians of my generation (back in the 1960s) chose to enter full time ministry, we were expected to have experienced what was termed, "The Call" to ministry, usually either to be a pastor or to be a missionary. We would be the ones with the greatest spiritual hunger and desire to lay down our lives to serve our King. Others would choose secular careers and could be "good Christians," but they would not have the same level of respect or honor in the church as those of us who had given up opportunities to make big money or climb the corporate ladder in order to fulfill "The Call."

We would be the ones that were looked on as having the most love for God, the greatest wisdom for counseling, the courage to witness and the patience to tolerate the smelly sheep. The lay people in the church would volunteer to serve the church and give their tithes and offerings so that the church could have a "pastor" available for weekly encouragement and special occasions like baptisms, marriages and funerals.

THE BIG ASSUMPTION ~ THE BIG LIE

It was from this paradigm that we all easily adopted the unspoken assumption that we, the clergy, had chosen to "seek first the Kingdom of Heaven." Others may be seeking first their own prosperity and security, but we, the called and chosen Levites, were definitely among those who were totally seeking first His Kingdom. Had we not left everything to follow Christ?

After almost fifty years in more or less "full-time ministry" I have to say from experience, that the answer is "NO!!!" No – most of us have not really forsaken all to follow Christ and, No – we have not always sought first the Kingdom of Heaven.

It is true that we have made sacrifices to follow Christ. Missionaries, especially in those days, had to say good-bye to loved ones for several years at a time. Children were taken back and forth from culture to culture, where they never felt like they really belonged. Many learned to adjust and be better for it, but it was not easy. Everyone who pastored or travelled in ministry also had things to let go of, and normal rights and freedoms were taken from them.

But does making some unusual sacrifice mean that we are seeking first God's Kingdom? I'd like to tell you some of my own story.

MY UNUSUAL CHILDHOOD

While you and I may excuse our lack of pure motives while we were growing up as something that was just normal for immature children, I have to say that I don't see a lot of difference in my own human nature as a child from my human nature as an adult. This is my story. Yours may be different, but everyone struggles with basically the same human weaknesses, when we really analyze ourselves honestly. We all want to be accepted, loved, affirmed and empowered. We want to look good and be seen as special. We want respect, honor, authority and power, and we don't want to be put down or embarrassed or made to look bad or stupid or ugly.

I have a few memories from early childhood relating to spiritual things. My parents were radical "Pentecostal Mennonites" who lived by faith, like few that I know of in my generation. They never asked for money and even turned down Canadian government family allowance checks to prove they were living by faith. They wanted above all else to have a clear conscience and please God, and they wanted each of their children to know God and His power, and to walk daily with Him.

They offered the same incentives to all their kids, but I was the one that took the greatest advantage of these incentives. There wasn't any specific financial reward for Bible reading that I can recall, but there was financial reward for memorizing Scripture. It started at one penny per verse and topped out at four pennies a verse, but it became my main source of income throughout my childhood.

Not only did I earn money for my "spiritual" prowess, but I also got attention and affirmation when I recited Scripture in church, Sunday School, or Daily Vacation Bible School. I won many contests, earned ranks in boys clubs, etc. One year at around the age of eleven, I memorized all twenty-three verses of Matthew 2, and recited it flawlessly at the church Christmas program. I overheard a lady telling my mother how amazing it was. That's all I needed to motivate me to do more.

Perhaps because I had two older brothers, who didn't seem to really value my ideas or suggestions, since I was the "little kid," I looked for attention from another group of people – the church. I would have loved to have more recognition for athletic achievement, but my athletic skills were never at the level that I could really impress the others in my class or peer group. I certainly could impress them in my dreams (both day and night dreams), but when it came to the games, themselves, I could never accomplish what I could in those wonderful dreams.

My academic achievements were almost always in the top three percent of my class, but to get major recognition would have been difficult. Being the most spiritual was easy for me, and that was the direction I chose – not consciously, of course, but obviously subconsciously.

Yes, I did love Jesus and I did experience His presence from time to time. I believed in God and the Bible, but my need for acceptance and honor were probably my primary motive. For the sake of bragging rights and self-satisfaction, I read through the Bible over and over and never skipped a "begat" or "the son of." I was very legalistic about telling the truth and wanted to have a clear conscience when I told someone I had read through the whole Bible.

If my memory is correct, I had read through every verse at least three times by the time I was ten years old. In addition, I had memorized nearly 1000 verses by the time I finished high school, without the benefit of a Christian school. I didn't know anyone else who had done what I had done, but although I was being prepared for my future ministry as a preacher and teacher of the Word of God, I would not say that I was totally motivated by a passion to build the Kingdom of Heaven on the earth.

Instead, my strongest motivation came from my love of accomplishment and the attention I received for it. I was the only kid that could answer almost all of the Bible questions, win Sword Drill competitions and any other awards that were given for Bible knowledge and memorization. I had found my niche and I loved the praise of men.

FROM CHILDHOOD TO EARLY MINISTRY YEARS

In Bible College, I had a powerful and totally life-changing personal encounter with God. I have shared more details in other books, especially *Humility and How I Almost Achieved It.* God truly gave me a passion to seek first His Kingdom, and I have lived in that passion to some extent throughout my decades of ministry.

However, as years passed, I became more and more cooperative with the prevailing mindset or paradigm regarding church and ministry. When I accepted the title, "Pastor" I accepted a responsibility and an understanding of my role in the church that was "normal" in our day, even though we were part of a "cutting edge" movement. Brenda and I were the pastors (shepherds) and we had people (God's sheep) that we needed to take care of. We would subconsciously ask ourselves the question, "What is expected of us in this situation?"

As a child I had been "spiritual" mostly for the sake of acceptance and recognition. Now as a young adult, I was being spiritual at least partly for the sake of acceptance and recognition as a pastor. I believed in all the Spiritual Gifts and wanted to demonstrate that I was a man of God, full of faith and power like Stephen. I wanted to be seen and known as someone who heard from God and whose prophetic words would truly come to pass.

In my mid-thirties, we planted a church in Washington State. We immediately had numerous visitors checking us out, and I had confidence we could accomplish great things. However, my desire to prove I could do this and that I was a strong prophetic preacher, motivated me to interpret some prophetic Scriptures to apply specifically to our region. I had received many true prophetic words in the past through Scripture, and I wanted to demonstrate this gift to our people. The problem was that some of the prophetic word was declaring economic judgment on our region. Deep inside, I wanted that judgment to happen so I would be vindicated as a man of God. There was some truth to the word and it did have a positive side, but my point here is that I was okay with the negative part, as long as I was vindicated.

Thus, even though I had experienced a life-changing encounter with God, and had received a passion for His church to be revived and restored, I had succumbed to the same pressure I had as a child to look spiritual. I was willing for others to suffer so that I would look good and would be honored as a true prophet. I wouldn't have verbalized or admitted it, but that was my heart. The drive to be seen as right or wise or spiritual mixed in with my love for God and His Kingdom.

BECOMING MORE OF A TRUE SPIRITUAL FATHER

After seven long years of slow growth in the church we planted, the pastor's nightmare happened. Most of our strongest families, including almost all the tithers and givers, had enough of my leadership, or lack thereof, and left for other churches. What followed was a season of brokenness and humbling as we sought God for direction and a way of escape from this obviously backward town that didn't recognize the gift God had given them. That gift, of course, was me.

Let me back up a little. We had been sent out by a larger church to plant the church with three families, two of whom had been driving a distance to attend the bigger church. While I ran a Christian school in a different neighboring town, we started meetings in the town that wanted to start a church under the covering of the bigger cutting-edge church in the bigger town. When the school year came to an end, we moved into that town, and then started our own Christian School, while starting the new church.

I was informed about the local ministerial association, and immediately attended the first monthly meeting. I don't remember much, except that I did size up the other pastors in the association. Many of the older traditional churches had tiny shriveling congregations with 10 to 15 members, with an average member age of about sixty or so. We already had more people in our church than they did. The pastors willing to serve these churches were for the most part ready to retire or just starting out with not much on their resumes.

There were a few larger churches, but even their pastors didn't seem to be very intimidating to me. I was a man on a mission to prove I was a man of God that could transform a small town through the power of the Holy Spirit in me. Incidentally, the other churches certainly were not excited about us being there. The town had already declined in population and most, if not all, of the churches had as well. They saw me as a threat to them. They also resented us for starting a Christian school and pulling out a few potential star athletes from the public schools.

Back to the ministerial meeting. As I looked the pastors over, I remember a thought crossing my mind that there didn't seem to be a lot of competition in the group. It wasn't that I wanted to have the biggest church in town, but I did hope we would be successful in attracting people to our "more anointed and cutting edge" church. Basically, I guess I was responding to the desire to "look good."

When the big split and loss occurred, it was a major wake-up call for us. I spent time seeking the Lord and asking if someone else could do a better job. I phoned a ministry leader, who ran a great Bible College to see if anyone was interested in taking it over. They had nobody interested. Then God clearly spoke to me directly, and also through an anointed prophet that I was not to leave.

A NEW BEGINNING

God did a work in my heart and I intentionally started to work on bringing unity in our community, praying regularly with other pastors for revival. This produced some special fruit that we had never seen before. Soon we were getting an influx of Mexican folk and we started a separate service in Spanish. I had a strong love affair with the Spanish people, language and culture, since my visit to Argentina in 1973, where, under our mentor, Elmer Burnette, I saw hundreds of healings and miracles and at least a thousand salvations in six weeks. That had been the most exciting time of my life and having a Spanish service with Spanish worship was a wonderful experience for me. God also sent some new people to help us with the English congregation, and we were enjoying a new level of God's presence in our meetings.

During this transition time, I was being revived and strengthened and reeducated in the concept of building the Kingdom of Heaven on earth, instead of building my own little kingdom and ministry. I knew that the only way to please God and agree with His heart was to care about every church, every pastor and every soul in the whole community.

God truly changed my heart, and when He finally released us from that church seven years later, He had given me a new heart and a new message for the church. I surely won't claim to have achieved perfection in this area, but I certainly have had a significant change of heart. I have much less need to prove myself to anyone today. I am God's child, loved and approved of and understood. He has given all for me. May I learn how to give my all for Him!

Oh that we could all forget what people think of us and just build God's Kingdom in His power and for His glory. And why not do it together, getting over ourselves and our reputation, etc. Let's find out how we fit into the team, without having to control everything and everyone to make sure that we look good.

THE IMPORTANT LESSON THE CHURCH HAS MISSED FROM SCRIPTURE

There are two stories in Scriptures that have a special message that the church has never noticed, as far as I know. Both stories take place when God was blessing His people with a brand new life in His Kingdom on the earth. The Old Testament story occurs as God begins to give Israel the keys to the Promised Land. The New Testament story occurs as God gives the church the keys to His power and victory over the enemy, in the early chapters of the Book of Acts.

1. Achan and Jericho.

God gave instructions for the battle they were facing and then He gave instructions for what to do after they had conquered Jericho. They were not to touch any of the spoils of war. That was all to be dedicated to God as the firstfruits of their blessings in the new land of promise. Achan was guilty of stealing and hiding silver and gold under his tent. But that was not the first thing he took. Notice his first words of confession:

"Indeed, I have sinned against the Lord God of Israel, and this is what I have done: When I saw among the spoils a beautiful Babylonian garment, two hundred shekels of silver, and a wedge of gold weighing fifty shekels, I coveted them and took them." (Joshua 7:20,21)

He declared, "When I saw among the spoils a beautiful Babylonian garment . . ." The first thing mentioned was a beauti-

17

ful and probably very expensive garment. Why did he covet the garment before the silver and gold? Simply this: HE WANTED TO LOOK GOOD!!! He and his poor family paid a terrible price for his actions.

2. Ananias and Sapphira.

Acts 5 tells the story of a couple of converts to Christianity, who saw how others were selling possessions and bringing the proceeds to the apostles. Obviously, people looked upon them with admiration for their great and generous sacrifice. As a result, Ananias and Sapphira sold some property themselves and brought some, but not all, of the proceeds to Peter and the apostles. They may not have intended to lie. They might have just wanted other people to assume that they had given it all. The result was disastrous for them as it was for Achan in Joshua's time. Peter, using the gift of knowledge, probed them to reveal their hearts, and they were both taken out that same day because of their deception.

Again, I ask, "Why did they do it?" The answer is simple: THEY WANTED TO LOOK GOOD.

I believe both these stories ended with very harsh judgment because God wanted to make a strong statement. Sin in the camp will bring death. His people were given a new start, a new life, but if they allowed sin in the camp, they would die. Both spiritual and natural death would come little by little, but the example was to be a warning to all.

Wanting to look good, in itself, may not be so bad. Certainly, we ought to dress to please the Lord and those we serve. But when that desire is motivated by pride and causes us to break God's laws, we can get ourselves into big trouble.

Today, God has allowed us more grace for this time of history. There may come a time again before Jesus returns, when, for the sake of the Kingdom of God, some selective harsh judgment may come to keep the church pure before His coming, but I'm thankful that He hasn't taken me out every time I wanted to look good and wasn't totally honest about it.

WHAT ARE YOU SEEKING?

Let me ask you the question, "What are YOU seeking? You have read my confession of what I was seeking in ministry. What would your story read like if you were writing this book? Are you still wanting to prove your natural or spiritual giftings and anointings? Have you been broken over your own deceptive heart, wanting to look good in front of others, and as a result, spending too much energy in building your own kingdom rather than God's?

I am reminded of the act of humbling and obedience that brought major blessings into my life. It was an act of letting my peers know my weakness and asking for prayer. My nineteen-year-old life took a whole new and wonderful course from that point on. Not only was I blessed with regular and powerful encounters with the Holy Spirit, but God brought my wonderful and amazing wife, Brenda into my life. Following that, I was the only one chosen to accompany our mentor to Argentina for the most explosive revival meetings that either of us had ever experienced. It was so worth it. I would do it a thousand times over to get the same results again. (For more of that story, check out *Humility, and How I Almost Achieved It.*

WHAT IS A KINGDOM-BUILDING CHURCH?

It's probably a good idea to define what we mean by a Kingdom-building church. Let's look at the way a natural kingdom is established and expanded.

» The king needs a palace – a place recognized as his home and the center of the kingdom.
» The king wants to secure and expand his borders with offensive and defensive weapons and armies.
» The king wants to bring in the wealth of other nations through trade and conquest.
» The king wants to have leaders so loyal to him that they will die to protect him. They must also be capable of administrating portions of his kingdom for him.
» The king wants subjects that will love him, serve him and be willing to fight for him.

1. Thus, the Kingdom-building church will build a palace of praise and worship, for He dwells in His temple, His body, the church, and He dwells in the praises of His people.
2. The Kingdom-building church will guard and expand the borders of the Kingdom – taking territory from the enemy and guarding the territory already under His domain from intruders.
3. The Kingdom-building church will bring the spiritual and natural riches and resources to provide for all the needs of the Kingdom – like we see happening in the early church.
4. The Kingdom-building church will equip leaders with pure and loyal hearts to use their gifts to administrate the

various aspects of the Kingdom. They will love not their own lives to the death.

5. The Kingdom-building church will impart the love of God to all its members, filling their hearts will passionate devotion for their King.

May God give us the wisdom and dedication to develop a Kingdom-building church like the one in the early chapters of the Book of Acts.

UNDERSTANDING BEING KINGS UNDER THE KING OF KINGS

In our book, *Kings and Kingdoms*, we learned that the King of kings desires to give us the privileges and responsibilities of being kings, serving the King of kings. We discussed how things were done in Jesus' time and for hundreds of years before and after. There was only one sovereign king on the earth. They usually called him the emperor or the caesar. But under him were many kings, who had been positioned to help him administrate his vast kingdom.

Jesus gave us a great parable illustrating this scenario in Luke 19:12-27. There He describes a certain nobleman who went into a far country to receive for himself a kingdom. In Jesus' day, they would have gone to Rome to the caesar. The nobleman would have had royal blood from previous generations of kings, like the Herod's in Judea. At any rate, he received his kingdom and then gave authority to his faithful servants to be kings over several cities, according to their stewardship abilities.

This concept is critically important to the subject of this book, because we need to understand that God does want to give us authority and honor, but we must first become fully dedicated and loyal servants, with only one goal. We want to bring honor and glory to Him, the King of kings and Lord of lords. Thus, I do highly encourage readers of this book to read Kings and Kingdoms as well.

Chapter 2

True Stories from People I Know

To make the point that we do need a major paradigm shift in the church today, from the church-building church, to the Kingdom-building church, I'd like to share some real life stories from personal friends and acquaintances, who have been affected by the current church growth paradigm. The real names and location of churches, pastors and church members are withheld for obvious reasons.

Jim

Let me start with someone I will call Jim. Jim was in the seminary program of a denominational school several decades ago. Some of the top leaders of that denomination came to visit the school and interview students and offer scholarship money to some of these top students. Jim was selected as one of those students and went to the interview. The leaders pressed Jim for a commitment that he would serve their denomination for a minimum of six years. The scholarship was for $600.00, a significant sum in the late 1960s. Jim said he could not promise to stay within the denomination, since he always sought for directions from God and didn't know what God had in mind that far into his future. The leaders were not happy with his answer. They shared their policy that Jim could keep $100.00 for every year he served the denomination, but if he left the denomination, he would have to return $100.00 per year of the first six that he didn't serve with their denomination. Jim agreed. After one or two years, Jim felt called to serve under an independent church pastor and faithfully began to repay the denomination of his seminary.

While Jim was serving as pastor within the denomination, he attended their regional pastors' conference. One of the clear instructions from the denominational leaders, who had come to speak at the conference, was that the pastors should instruct their people not to support other mission organizations, since they couldn't trust where their money was going unless they gave to their own church missions program.

Of course, church leaders could feel totally justified and make their case for these kinds of practices, based on the fact that some of the other churches or missions to serve or support might be not as theologically correct or as financially integral. However, what Jim heard in his own spirit, was that these men were more concerned about the growth and success of their own denomination than they were with the advancement of the Kingdom of Heaven on Earth.

Fred

Fred had been a pastor and marriage counselor for a number of years. One summer he led a team to Mozambique and saw God's power displayed in wonderful ways. Later that summer, he was speaking at a church camp, as he did every year. He challenged the youth to go on the mission's trip to the same field with him the next year. He knew they would get excited about the power of God and have their own deep encounters with God. Many young people got excited about the opportunity. Fred was not aware that the church supported their own missions program in another African country and were trying to recruit young people to go on a mission trip there.

The reaction from the church leaders was not very kind. They told him that if they had known what he would be speaking about, they would not have asked him to speak. If kids from their church wanted to go on a mission trip, they should go to the field that their church was supporting.

When I heard about this situation, I thought about the concept of building the Kingdom as opposed to building our own ministry. I'm sure the ministry and the kids would have been blessed if they had gone on their own church's mission trip, but they probably wouldn't have experienced the same "book of Acts" type of results that would get them super excited about God and building His Kingdom. What if just one young person would be impacted to seek God for His power and character like we had witnessed by the leadership of the ministry in Mozambique? What if that one person became an anointed missionary or evangelist, bringing tens of thousands of souls to Christ?

Because of the negative reaction, I'm not sure any of the youth went to either field to build the Kingdom. I could be wrong, but I felt like there was a missed opportunity for a church organization to put the Kingdom before their own ministry.

It's my belief that until we actually sacrifice our own ministry to help someone else's ministry, we might question whether we are really seeking His Kingdom before our own ministry.

Natalie (In Her Own Words)

The Lord led me to start a discipleship school in a large church of about 6000 members. The vision and purpose of this school was to train teachers through the curriculum of another cutting-edge ministry. After two years, we presented it as a one-year program to the whole congregation. Over one thousand students of all ages and walks of life completed the program. Many were missionaries according to the spiritual gifts tests which were performed. Some were pastors and leaders in the community. Nearly two thirds of the students, over a seven-year period, were attending different churches in the community. This was so exciting, as the vision given me was for a school that would minister to the whole community.

After the foundational program, I introduced an advanced level discipleship school to equip the believers to maturity to help fulfill the great commission. This was composed of worship, prayer, revelatory teaching and outreach projects. The fruit was huge and the anointing increased to amazing transformations. The Kingdom Spirit-led lifestyle was the message and demonstration. God's dream was happening. It was ready to go to the next level. However, one evening I invited the pastor to come speak on the Kingdom. Soon after I was called into the Pastor's office with two other staff pastors. I was also on staff. I was required to stop the discipleship class and to be more "in House". From that time on I was stifled from fulfilling the assignment God had given me.

It was dark days of betrayal, pain and hardship until the Lord released me to leave and to start a new ministry, which became an equipping church and an apostolic work in Africa. I finally left the large church with the lead pastor's blessing, in spite of all the difficulties that had transpired. God deserves all the Glory for it.

The School of Discipleship was to equip believers in the maturity of Kingdom Spirit-led living, to empower them in the Supernatural, the prophetic anointing, and to send them forth in what God had purposed in their life. There was an interdenominational anointing and an international anointing on this God dream. It was to advance the Kingdom, be supported by a church, and reach out to the community and the world. And it was so close to reaching a place of fullness when it was made to end so abruptly.

Author's Comments: What Natalie experienced was the disapproval of a ministry that was helping to empower people of other churches, rather than just their own. I believe this breaks the heart of God. Whose kingdom are we building? His or ours, or a little of both?

Robert and Katie

Robert and his wife, Katie, also became part of a large church, which had been built mostly on the charisma of the pastor. This pastor was well known and had planted a number of satellite churches, as well as the one where he lived. The message of the church was mostly a message of earthly prosperity and how to get the things you desire from God.

Everything looked appealing and positive from a distance, but as Robert and Katie got offered positions in the leadership, including worship, they began to see things that didn't add up. Before long, they found out the pastor's wife was afraid of her husband and ended up hiding with them for a short time. They had gone to meet her and discovered that the mansion of a home the pastor and his wife lived in was almost totally empty on the inside. It was a show home, but like their ministry it was more show than reality, for it was a shell with little happiness or substance within it.

This young couple was very disappointed and confused about what ministry was all about. However, a prophetic friend of ours gave them a word, never having met them, and God reassigned them to another, more Kingdom-minded ministry.

Their situation was rather extreme, but not unique. Building or growing a local church or a mega church ministry can be done with human talent and some truth mixed in, but God is looking for those who have laid down their own ambitions and are willing to labor in this world for a future reward, not the praise of men in this life.

A SIGN THAT MADE ME WONDER

Yes, it was a church sign which caught my attention. Normally, church signs have service times and other information about the church. Others will also have some clever statement or Scripture verse. This one clearly demonstrated a church-building church. It said, "We don't use hype, we just teach the Bible."

Now why would they say that they don't use hype? It was obvious if you lived in the neighborhood. There was a newer and fast growing church down the street that used drama, cutting edge technology and worship music along with well-prepared, time-sensitive sermons to reach those that wouldn't come to a traditional church service. It was the church that you would want to invite an unbeliever or "pre-Christian" to attend to hear about salvation and the Kingdom of Heaven.

Obviously, there was a spirit of jealousy and a critical spirit being released from the church with the sign. They were tired of watching another church grow, probably at their own expense, and they put up their flesh-exposing sign. Lest I reveal my own critical spirit, may I hasten to add, that as a pastor, I've also responded in my preaching to churches that build their ministries with natural entertainment, etc.

But the problem is, this is not an isolated problem. It is closer to epidemic proportions, and it's time we realized it. And it's not that these pastors are bad people, or don't love Jesus. They just get used to the idea that they are in competition with other churches, and if they don't build their church, no one else will. They feel the pain of loss of members and loss of income. They want to fight back at the injustice of someone stealing their sheep.

The question we should all ask ourselves is this: Do I get excited when another ministry prospers and people are finding Jesus, especially when my ministry is struggling to stay alive or pay its bills? Or do I try to discredit the other ministry for not being as pure as ours?

Another question we should ask ourselves would be: What have I ever done to sacrifice myself or my own ministry to help another ministry that might be struggling with human or financial resources, without expecting something in return? These are questions that help us reveal how much we have a Kingdom-First mentality and how much we have a My-Church-First mentality.

May God truly enlighten us and reveal our hearts to us, so that He can both heal and refill our hearts with a fresh passion to build His Kingdom and let Him build His church like He said He would.

Chapter 3

Our Best Example

As far as I am concerned, we have no better documented example of a Kingdom-building church than the story of the early church, as recorded in the book of Acts. Let's take a fresh look at this church from this point of view. How did they put building the Kingdom before building their own ministries and churches?

1. Total Dependence on the Holy Spirit

My perspective is that the church was at its high point spiritually at the beginning, even though it did not fully understand the fullness of God's grace for the Gentiles. The first church was led by the disciples of Jesus. He had graduated them to be apostles in John 20:21, when He said, "As the Father has sent me, so send I you." Apostle means "sent one."

These apostles had just experience the amazing grace of their amazing Savior and Redeemer. They were clearly guilty of desertion and forsaking their Commander in Chief in the heat of the battle just before the cross. Undoubtedly, they felt like the greatest failures that ever lived, and probably had mixed emotions about the possibility of seeing Jesus alive again. They obviously deserved to be harshly punished by their Master, but instead, Jesus spoke "Shalom" twice and then uttered the words "As the Father has sent Me, so send I you, thus totally forgiving them, and in fact, promoting them to their life's mission and its corresponding spiritual authority.

After this incredible experience, they were no longer jockeying for position in Jesus' Kingdom. Now they had one passion – to bring back the King by taking the gospel to the whole world. They would obey His commands and tarry in Jerusalem, until they had the same Holy Spirit that empowered their Teacher/ Messiah. For the first time in their history, we are told they were "in one accord." And that was before the Holy Spirit fell upon them. As Jesus had spoken to them earlier, "He who is forgiven much, loves much." The apostles were well aware of how much they had been forgiven, and they loved much more after their failure than they did before.

Their brokenness and true humility released a wave of passionate devotion and commitment to Jesus and His Kingdom. I believe this passion came to a high note at the ascension of Jesus.

Imagine being one of the eleven disciples, who had been with Jesus for at least three years. Imagine the feelings of failure after the cross, and then the surge of love and devotion to Him after He appeared to you in His resurrected body and spoke, "Shalom!" to you. Imagine the excitement of anticipation that He would now set up His Kingdom.

Then imagine after forty days seeing Him again in Jerusalem

and asking Him if this was the time that He would take the throne of Israel. Then you hear Him tell you that it was not the time for that, but that you would receive power after the Holy Spirit had empowered you and you would be His witnesses to the ends of the earth.

Then, suddenly, His feet are no longer touching the ground and He is looking down on you with love in His eyes and waving good bye, rising higher and higher until He disappears into the clouds. Imagine the wave of emotions sweeping over your soul. First a measure of disappointment, then sadness at His departure, then loneliness, then deep, deep love, then determination to not disappoint Him and then excitement for the assignment and the promise He had made to you.

Your eyes continue to gaze into the clouds, hoping for one last glimpse of the One who gave His life for you and then so graciously forgave you for deserting Him in His hour of need. Suddenly, you're aware of the presence of holy beings beside you. Dressed in white, these beautiful angels declare that He will be coming back, just the way He departed. You have no idea when that will be, but you hope it will be soon, and you are determined to do anything and everything in your power to hasten that event.

Can you imagine how you would undergo a major paradigm shift in your approach to ministry? Would you care who had the most prestigious position in your religious organization, or would you just be thrilled to be on His team, doing whatever He allowed you to do to advance His Kingdom and hasten His return? I believe I know what your answer would be.

But the most significant point about what you would have gone through in that experience is that you would know what a failure you are in your own strength and you would embrace the promise that the Holy Spirit will come to lead you and empower you to do the works of your Master. After all, that's why you become a disciple in the first place. You want to do the same things that your Master does. Now He has commissioned you as His disciple, to do just that, taking His power and love to the ends of the earth. You are promised that when that has taken place He will return in the clouds. You have an assignment and a promise that His Holy Spirit will empower you. You will gladly wait in Jerusalem until that promise is fulfilled.

2. A Church Experiencing the Awesome Blessings of Incredible Unity

In answer to Jesus' prayer in John 17, God had orchestrated the events that would cause the young apostles to have a strong enough passion to overpower their flesh and bring about the unity needed to facilitate a mighty move of the Spirit of God. As we read in Psalm 133, God commands a blessing where there is unity. Let's take a quick tour through this loaded three-verse chapter.

> *"Behold how good and how pleasant it is for brethren to dwell together in unity."*

The word dwell means more than getting along for an hour or two on Sunday. It really means to spend time living and working together. How awesome and fun it is when it truly happens that we can enjoy each other when we spend a lot of time together. When that happens, God commands that we be blessed.

"It is like the precious oil upon the head, running down on the beard, the beard of Aaron, running down on the edge of his garments."

This may not make any sense at first glance, but hold on a second. This is a powerful word about unity. After all, only Aaron was anointed by Moses to be the High Priest, and this was a very costly and precious oil for a very important ceremony. What God is saying here is that dwelling together in unity gives us a similar anointing as Aaron had.

The anointing was for the privilege and responsibility of coming before the holy presence of God Almighty and interceding on behalf of the people. Aaron was able to make atonement for the people and bring them into favor with God so that their sins could be forgiven. This is similar to what we are allowed and anointed to do on behalf of others when we are walking in this kind of unity. That's a blessing that God commands to be ours.

"It is like the dew of Hermon, descending upon the mountains of Zion; for there the Lord commanded the blessing – Life forevermore."

The dew of Hermon represents blessings of provision. Without the dew, the plant life on the mountain might die in the desert sun. But the moisture condenses during the cold night and waters the vegetation, producing food for the hungry, be it man or beast. Likewise, unity provides the blessings of provision.

How did this blessing manifest in the early church? They certainly dwelt together in unity. Acts records five times in the first five chapters that the church was in "one accord." This was

God's fulfillment of the prayer of Jesus in John 17, when He prayed five times that His disciples would be "one." We should thus see these blessings manifested there in obvious ways.

The first blessing of unity in community mentioned in Psalm 133, was the High Priestly anointing to bring forgiveness of sins to others. Did this happen in the early church? Yes, it surely did in a powerful way. In fact, the anointing that fell on the church at Pentecost was so powerful that it first caused them all to speak supernaturally in foreign languages, and then Peter preached a spontaneous message that caused the people to cry out for forgiveness. Peter, still manifesting the High Priestly anointing, led them to repent and receive the wonderful promise of the Holy Spirit in their lives. In a moment, three thousand men had their sins forgiven by God.

That all happened in Chapter Two of Acts. In Chapter three, the anointing was strong enough to bring about the healing of a forty year-old man, who was born a cripple and had never walked. The crowd gathered and Peter preached another message calling for repentance, and when the dust settled, the number of men in the brand new church had reached five thousand.

When you estimate how many women and children were also included in the church, it could have been well over twenty thousand. Not a bad start for a new church plant, considering that there were no transferring members from other churches. Every new member was a brand new baby Christian. The High Priestly anointing was manifesting in great power and might.

The second blessing of unity was the dew of Hermon or provision in desert seasons. Here again we see a most beautiful example of the fulfillment of Psalm 133. The early church, like nothing we have ever seen, lived together in unity, as described in Acts 4:32-35:

"Now the multitude of those who believed were of one heart and one soul; neither did anyone say that any of the things he possessed was his own, but they had all things in common. And with great power the apostles gave witness to the resurrection of the Lord Jesus. And great grace was upon them all.

Nor was there anyone among them who lacked; for all who were possessors of lands or houses sold them, and brought the proceeds of the things that were sold, and laid them at the apostles' feet; and they distributed to each as anyone had need."

Clearly, we see how unity facilitated provision for all. This was a powerful and wonderful blessing that God commanded, through the work of the Holy Spirit moving on them to love one another with practical demonstrations of kindness and generosity.

First of all, we read that people who owned real estate put their houses and lands on the market and brought the sales price to the apostles. That would be a significant amount of cash. Secondly, we are told that no one was left out when it came to participating in the resources. Truly, as the dew of Hermon was making provision for every blade of grass on the mountain, so the provision from the body of Christ was there for every man, woman and child that made up the body of Christ.

3. Having Been with Jesus Gave the Apostles Kingdom Hearts

While they were Jesus' disciples, the apostles had learned many things, not the least of which was how much compassion

Jesus had for the weak and despised members of society. They also learned that He was a strong and fearless leader, taking on the kingpins of their religious society and knocking over the tables of the money-changers in the temple.

But, although they had seen His example, and knew what He might do in any given situation, they had no inner power to do what He did until they had been filled with the same Holy Spirit that He had operated in. That was when the apostles could truly function like Jesus had, since they had been given the same power He had been given by the Holy Spirit.

Thus, when the rulers of Israel interrogated the apostles, Peter turned things around and put the rulers on the witness stand, accusing them of murdering the very Messiah they had been waiting for. The leaders noticed the boldness of the apostles and they *"marveled and they realized that they had been with Jesus."*

Having been with Jesus and then having been filled with the same Holy Spirit, the apostles had hearts for Jesus and His Kingdom. Jesus was constantly talking about the Kingdom of Heaven and it had become a part of their DNA. Their mandate was not to build a church – Jesus had told them that it was His job to build His church. Their mandate was to expand and build His Kingdom, through His power. Jesus had given them that authority after His resurrection. The church, the body of Christ would be the instrument that God would use to build His Kingdom.

4. The Apostles Were Aware of Their Varying Gifts

Having overcome their need to be more important than the others, each apostle allowed the others to fulfill their own individual roles in the church and Kingdom. Obviously, Peter was the natural leader and did most of the public speaking. But John was usually at his side and supported him, probably with a strong gift of faith.

James, the brother of Jesus, seemed to be an administrative apostle, though not one of the original twelve. Phillip was an evangelist and performed many miracles in Samaria, where many conversions occurred. But Peter and John came to Samaria to bless the converts with the filling or baptism of the Holy Spirit. Phillip, apparently was not a "specialist" in getting people filled with the Holy Spirit, but Peter and John were.

Soon seven deacons were chosen to help with the administration of food distribution, etc. The first one mentioned was Stephen, a young man who was full of faith and the power of the Holy Spirit. He was also anointed to do great miracles among the people and was creating such a stir that the religious leaders had him stoned to death.

In Acts 13, we read that there were certain prophets and teachers in the church at Antioch. They were recognized by their gifts and functions in the body of Christ. But none of them were trying to use their gifts to build their own ministries. There was only one church in every city, and everyone knew their part, because their mandate was to expand the Kingdom of Heaven on the earth, not to build a new and unique ministry, based on their functioning gifts.

Also, in Acts 13, we read that the Holy Spirit spoke and called for Barnabas and Saul to be set apart for special ministry. My assumption is that one or more of the prophets present were used by the Holy Spirit to make that call. At any rate, the two of them were sent out as the first missionaries to go to lands far beyond the borders of Israel.

In Acts 21:8-10, we read again of Philip, the evangelist, who had four virgin daughters who prophesied, and then we read of Agabus, the prophet, who had prophesied earlier of a coming famine, and now warned Paul about what awaited him in Jerusalem.

The point we can clearly see from this, is that every member of the body was fulfilled in doing what they were called to do. They were full of passion to prepare the earth for the return of the King. They longed for His return and they had no need to do their own thing and get recognition from men as to how successful they were in building their ministry bigger and stronger than the one down the street.

5. The Apostles Had Little Emphasis on Church Buildings

Most of the ministry of the early church, as far as we can tell, happened outdoors, not in a building. Ministry was done where the people were. They didn't fish in their own swimming pool, they went to the lake where the fish were. They weren't worried about where the fish would become members. They were all part of the same church of the city, and were okay with that.

Today, it's hard to conceive of a "real" church without a building with a name on it. We can't imagine church life without a gathering place, a center of activities, yet the early Jerusalem church was composed of thousands of believers who, we are told, were all together and in unity, but we are not told where they were meeting, other than the Jewish temple or synagogues at the beginning. These were certainly not Christian church buildings, as the rabbis and scribes and Pharisees were in control of these buildings and could expel people from attending them.

We are told that they fellowshipped from house to house and later, in the epistles of Paul, we read four times about the church in people's homes. (Romans 16:5, I Corinthians 16:19, Colossians 4:15, Philemon 1:2) Certainly, one could not get thousands of people in one house, so we know that the people from the one church of the city must have met in many different homes, perhaps gathering sometimes in fields or parks, but archaeologists have found no record of actual Christian church buildings in the first three hundred years of church history. Church buildings were built after the Roman emperor, Constantine, made Christianity the state religion of the Roman Empire.

Of course, before that time, Christians were persecuted by the Romans and therefore would not have been free to own property for church buildings. However, in spite of this handicap, the church continued to grow and build the Kingdom of Heaven on the earth, without building any cathedrals or centers of operations. This is truly remarkable, but consistent with the New Testament church paradigm. Church was all about being excited about Jesus and going to where the people were who needed to hear the good news of the Kingdom of Heaven coming to earth.

Having a church building is not a bad thing in itself, but there are dangers we should be aware of.

First, it gives us a feeling of identity, which can increase our ability to separate ourselves from other churches. This is our church. We are different from the other churches. Inside our building, we don't need to identify with other Christians. We can stay in our comfort zones with people like ourselves who believe and worship just like we do.

In recent meetings where pastors from an Indiana town were sharing, they mentioned how they had been living so close to other pastors, but never got to know them. Revival had brought a unity they had never experienced and they were now praying together on a regular basis. As many as ninety pastors had gathered in the same place to pray together. Pastors of churches with greatly divergent church backgrounds were learning to worship with each other and loving it. It wasn't their buildings that had actually separated them. It was their pride in their own doctrine or tradition, but the buildings helped facilitate their separation.

Secondly, we feel pressure to maintain and finance our building. When finances get tight, we still have to make our mortgage payments. Leaders fear losing their tithers, lest they lose their building. It motivates them to keep their people happy at almost any cost, and sometimes it influences their decisions and the messages they preach.

Thirdly, it causes us to focus our time and energy, as well as our finances, on a material possession, which may rob us of resources which could be used to evangelize or bless missionaries, etc. I have seen statistics that house churches, which do not usually have to pay church salaries or mortgage payments, give far more to missions per capita than typical churches that have a church facility. I don't remember the source, but it does make sense. Again, there are pro's and con's to both arrangements, but these are things worth thinking about.

Fourthly, it becomes so easy to call the building, "the church." This is a serious problem, because it makes people think they can "Go to church" instead of being the church. The church is the living, breathing, working organism that is the actual body of Jesus Christ, The Anointed One. It is redeemed people, using their God-given abilities and spiritual gifts and fruit, that carry the anointing of The Anointed One. It is not a building – it's you and it's me. Although it's a tough habit to break, I try to never call a building "the church." I usually refer to it as a church's facility or a sanctuary, set apart for worship, or a center for church activities, but it definitely is NOT the church.

NOTE: Buildings are not the problem, and if we are conscious of the dangers we mentioned above, they can be a wonderful blessing, especially if we share them with others in the Kingdom. The real problem, of course, is our pride in wanting to be more special than others in the city or town we serve.

SUMMING UP

To wrap up this chapter, let's see if we can make sense of what we've observed about the early church.

1. There was a very vibrant and controlling dynamic. It was the apostles' awareness of their own failures and weaknesses and their knowledge that the power of the Holy Spirit was in them to do the same work that Jesus had done. They were His representatives, His "sent ones," who had a mandate to build His Kingdom in all the earth.

2. They loved Jesus with all their hearts and saw Him as their King, who had to remain in Heaven until they had carried the good news about His Kingdom into all the earth. They had passion and were in unity. Nothing on earth mattered much to them. It was all about bringing Jesus back to earth. Unity was easy, since they were all in love with Jesus and wanted the same thing – to build His Kingdom and to bring Him back to earth.

3. They had Kingdom hearts because they had been with

Jesus. Jesus talked about the Kingdom all the time and that was their focus. He talked very little about the church and how it should work, etc. He was laying the foundation. The rest was up to the apostles to learn how to administrate the church. I believe those who spend time with Jesus today in worship, prayer and the Word, will also develop a Kingdom Heart and lose their personal ambition to build a ministry to honor their own greatness and giftings.

4. They recognized they were created with different gifts and abilities. They knew where they fit and how to work as part of a team. There was only one church in the city and they found their place in that one church.

5. Finally, not having their own church buildings did not stop them from building the Kingdom of Heaven on the earth. They did not call any building the church. They knew that THEY WERE the church and they were called to share their wonderful news about the coming King and His Kingdom with everyone everywhere. They were getting things ready on the earth for the coming of the King to take His throne and rule in righteousness.

The previous five characteristics of the early church are those that are obvious to me. Perhaps you see others that facilitated a Kingdom mindset. But I do believe that when we begin to see more and more of these same five characteristics in the church of today, we know we are getting closer to the return of Jesus.

In the following pages, we want to share some essential keys and some practical suggestions to transform our lives and ministries from being church-centered to being Kingdom-centered.

Chapter 4

Prescription for Transformation

In this chapter, we will offer several steps to bring about a paradigm shift to the church of the twenty-first century, not just the western church, but also churches of every nation. Sadly, some of our flawed western attitudes and methods have been freely exported to other nations. We are hopeful that through a powerful revival and awakening in our generation, the Holy Spirit will enlighten His whole church and empower us to put His Kingdom before our own ministry and success.

Here are the steps I believe church leaders can take to make the twenty-first century church more like the first century church – A Kingdom-building church.

1. Ask God to Search Your Heart and Be Brutally Honest with You.

I know you that you probably ask God to search your heart

on a regular basis, but let me encourage you to view this process differently than you would normally. Instead of thinking, "Well, maybe I've messed up without realizing it," or "Maybe I shouldn't have said or done such and such," let's take this approach:

"Lord, I know my flesh is my enemy and yours. I know I don't have enough of your character and your nature to respond correctly to the challenges I face every day. I know I grieve your Holy Spirit. I know my pride stinks and it causes you to resist me. Please, God, don't let me do the things that offend you without bringing me under conviction. And God, because I want to be a Kingdom builder, and my church to be a Kingdom-building church, please show me where I've been putting my ministry ahead of your Kingdom, because I've wanted to look good to other people. It's been so easy to fall into that trap and justify it, because everyone else seems to be doing it too."

At this point, I want to share something that is very heavy on my heart and I am passionately convinced that this is heavy on the heart of God as well. In recent weeks, especially the last two weeks or so, I have shared some truths about the importance and power of true humility. Every time I have shared in groups large or small, I have felt a stronger than normal anointing and emotion welling up in me.

I have learned over the past few years that God loves to manifest His emotions as well as His truths through human vessels. When I got emotional about something I was sharing with a large group, God told me it was because He was also emotional about that particular subject or situation in the church. It had to do with people never being encouraged to unwrap the gifts He had given them or to use them to bless one another.

So when I began to feel the deep emotion of the Father's

heart on the subject of humility, I paid attention and listened to the Holy Spirit for more clarification. Each time I shared on the subject, God would give me more and more insights and revelation. Finally, I received what I believe is a very significant truth that constantly weighs heavy on the heart of God.

When the Bible tells us that God resists the proud, but gives grace to the humble, it is a principle or "spiritual law" that God will not overrule. He has also shown me clearly that most manifestations of the flesh, like anger, self-pity, greed, jealousy, resentment, bitterness, etc., are deeply rooted in pride. (I deal with that in greater detail in my book called, Humility and How I Almost Achieved it.)

Therefore, whenever I am arguing or angry or feeling sorry for myself, etc., I am manifesting pride. That means that God must resist me in those moments. If I'm fighting with my spouse, no matter who's right, we're both wrong if we're defending ourselves and attacking the other. We are manifesting pride. Only by pride comes contention. (Prov. 13:10)

What makes the Father so sad is that He must resist us instead of giving us grace. While He is Himself resisting us, the enemy has free access to us. God can't resist and take our side at the same time. That's why we find ourselves saying and doing things that we so regret later. We have yielded to the enemy through our pride and lost our divine protection. This is a scary thought for us, but it is a very sad thing for our Heavenly Father. Every father wants to defend and protect his own children. To have to resist us breaks His heart.

Thus, we would be very wise to ask God to convict us and help us to humble ourselves as quickly as possible. His promises are amazing for those who humble themselves. These promises include His abiding presence, revival and healing for our land, honor and authority and of course, grace. These promises and more should be motivation enough for us to capture every opportunity to humble ourselves. Lovingly, God presents these to us on a regular basis every day.

2. Dont' Compromise Passion to Bring Unity.

We all know that God wants unity far more than we who are Christians seem to want it. As we mentioned earlier, Jesus prayed for it five times in one passionate prayer before Calvary, in John 17. It seems then that we should do everything possible to help fulfill that prayer in our churches today.

The natural thinking person would say, "Well, it's our doctrines that divide us. Therefore, we need to compromise some and be less dogmatic about our doctrines. Then we can have greater unity." There is an element of truth to that thought, but it is based on a false assumption, which I will address shortly.

Another thought might be, "Well, it's the way we worship or pray that offends others, so we'll just modify our worship and prayer, so we can have greater unity." Again, there is an element of truth to that, but it again is based on a wrong assumption about unity and division.

Debunking False Assumptions

The first assumption is that our doctrines divide us. That seems to be the case, since that's what so many theologians and church leaders have argued about over the centuries. But we have been looking at the surface causes of disunity, rather than the root causes.

Here is the truth as I see it:

We are not divided because of different doctrines. We are divided because of our pride in our doctrines – our pride in being right and wanting to look good.

If we all took a humility pill and asked the Holy Spirit to help us understand each other, we might more clearly hear His voice. If we acknowledged that the founder of our denomination, or movement, got some great revelations, but perhaps he or she didn't get everything exactly right, we could be on the right track. Perhaps God saved some insights and revelations for others who would come after him or her.

The truth is that God will not give all truth and wisdom and knowledge to any one particular leader. We are the body of Christ and we all are called on to contribute. Jesus is the only Head of that body, and He dispenses His truth and revelation to different ones, whom He chooses to steward His treasures in a spirit of humility, and not in a spirit of pride.

I don't believe anyone has got all their eschatology (study of end times events) perfect yet. God won't give all the truth to those who think they can figure it out through scholarship and logic. Otherwise, the Scribes and Pharisees would have recognized Jesus as the Messiah. I hear too many eschatology "experts" making too many statements of fact, when they are no more than theories.

God reveals His secrets to those who love Him, not to the best scholars. Scholarship is helpful and a worthy endeavor, but pride is the killer. As Paul declared, "Knowledge puffs up." Those who are scholars need to be especially on guard for pride of knowledge, lest they find God resisting them and hiding His knowledge from them.

But back to the concept of unity. There is no unity without humility and although we can agree to disagree, true unity is being able to dwell together and to work together with a common passion to accomplish God's goals, not our own. Therefore, real unity will never come from modifying our doctrines to reduce our differences with others.

The second false assumption is that we can have unity if we modify the way we worship so we won't offend those that do it differently. Although it's true that we can turn people off by getting weird, whether in the Spirit or in the flesh, it's also true that by not doing those things we still don't achieve unity. We just give others a little less to criticize. The danger is that we often don't want to offend people for the wrong reasons. We don't want to scare them away from our ministry. But when we suppress the joy or passion that God gave us, we also suppress His presence and we turn other people away who are actually looking for the passion and fire of the Holy Spirit.

I am not saying that when we get together with other believers, outside our own religious environment, who worship differently, that we should make a show of how we do it. We need to be sensitive to the Holy Spirit and ask Him how to properly love those we are with. He will guide us if we are more concerned about pleasing Him and helping others than with being right or "spiritual."

How then do we help facilitate the fulfillment of the prayer of Jesus that we would all become one? This is what I firmly believe:

We become one in true unity by getting so intimately and passionately in love with Jesus that we only want to make Him known and build His Kingdom on this earth. When our love is so strong and our hearts are so truly humble and grateful for His love, it's then that He can download His power and authority into our lives.

When we walk in His power and authority, in true humility, not trying to draw attention to ourselves or our own ministries, we will first attract others of like Spirit, and then we will attract others who want what we have. This is where true unity will have its very powerful effect.

When we are humbly, yet joyfully, healing the sick, raising the dead and setting people free from demonic control, controversial doctrines will not be on the minds of the people, nor will styles of worship keep the needy away. The common people will come to receive, while ministry leaders will humble themselves and want to participate in the revival. It happened in Jesus' time and in the early church. Even some Pharisees believed in Jesus when they saw the signs and wonders. I've also witnessed it firsthand.

In 1973, I had the privilege of accompanying our beloved mentor, Elmer Burnette, to Argentina, where we were hosted by Jack Schissler and his wife, Miriam. Jack had been working for years with a number of pastors, but it seemed they were always upset with each other, filled with jealousy and bitterness. But Jack Schissler had a Bible School filled with radical lovers of Jesus. When I heard them worship, it was unlike anything I'd ever heard – so intimate, so pure and heart-felt.

The students were the prayer team, and had been preparing for these meetings with months of prayer and fasting. In fact, they alternated days when they would eat and when they would fast. The girls fasted one day and the boys the next. They were very glad when we arrived and they could get back to eating every day.

When the first two meetings, in a modest-sized church, produced some amazing miracles, the word got out to all the churches that had worked with Jack. When we moved to a large auditorium, all the pastors showed up. But before the meetings progressed, we witnessed pastors humbling themselves and confessing their attitudes towards each other. They wept and hugged and sat on the platform together. They joined the Bible School students and helped pray for the sick and those coming for salvation.

There in Argentina, doctrines weren't an issue and neither was the way we worshipped. The worship was very different. Choruses were repeated dozens of times, while people seemed lost in the Spirit, worshipping with tears streaming down their faces. It was just awesome and paved the way for amazing miracles every night.

Much more recently, I was blessed to hear first-hand reports from the fresh new revival happening in Indiana, which I referred to in an earlier chapter. The revival began when an Amish man asked God to revive his people. God began to move on the Amish and soon other pastors and their flocks were attracted to the move of God. Before long there were up to ninety pastors meeting together for united prayer. I heard the testimonies of pastors from different denominations, and how they had always avoided the others, not realizing what they were missing by remaining isolated from each other.

No church had to change its official doctrine or style of worship, but they found out their "competition" was not at all as bad as they might have thought.

The unity God wants has little to do with doctrine or style of worship – it has everything to do with loving Him and working together for the same goals. It's about a common passion, which is much more than just a desire. For more information on the subject of passion versus desire, please read *Holy Passion - Desire on Fire.*

3. Appeal to Leaders Under and Over You.

If you happen to be in a position where you can see it is obvious that the ministry you're involved in is more interested in building itself than in building the Kingdom of God, what can you do to change that? You may be under someone else's authority, and/or you may be in authority over other leaders who have their own agenda.

The Godly appeal is still the best advice for anyone in such a position. If that doesn't have any effect, then some stronger action needs to be taken. So, what is a Godly appeal?

For Someone Over You

If you are under authority in a church or ministry and you feel you are being used to advance an agenda other than to build the Kingdom of Heaven, you should carefully and prayerfully prepare an appeal to the person over you.

Before going to the person with your appeal, however, you need to apply steps one and two above. You must ask God to highlight your own selfish motives and ambitions and repent of the manifestations of pride that you deal with on a regular basis. Secondly, you need to ask God for a passion for unity, like Jesus demonstrated in John 17, as did Paul in many of his epistles.

If your own heart is prepared with humility and a passion for unity, you will be able to present the most effective appeal. This appeal must be presented as a humble suggestion as to how to accomplish greater things for God, through applying some neglected biblical principles. The quickest way to be rejected is to come across as knowing better or being more spiritual than your leaders.

Your humble appeal should include a testimony of your own failures in related issues to the ones you will bring up, as well as the grace that God extended to you in forgiving you for your carnal motives. You might share the Scriptures that God used to convict you, and then also ask forgiveness from those over you in the ministry, acknowledging that your wrong motives have hindered the ministry from being blessed by God.

Then, if your confession is well received, you may mention that you sometimes feel the ministry puts too much emphasis on growing itself instead of finding more opportunities to help other ministries and build unity in the Christian community. You might share a story or two of what has happened in other communities, like in Indiana, where pastors began to support each other and pray for each other. The people would team up and go witnessing together and a great harvest was taking place. As they sacrificed their own ministries to serve others, they all got blessed by God.

End your appeal in a respectful and submissive spirit, thanking them for listening to you and asking them to pray about these concerns. Acknowledge that you know that they have a lot of burdens and decisions and a lot of people offering advice. Your purpose is not to add to their burden, but to encourage them for greater Kingdom results.

If You Have Leaders Serving Under You

If you are an overseer of other people's ministries and you see them striving to make themselves known or are motivated by personal ambition in any way, you can use the same basic principles as we discussed above. Don't speak down to them or make them feel judged. Let them know about your own journey and how God has had to discipline you for your flesh. Acknowledge that everyone needs affirmation, and sometimes we get it from the way that people respond to how we perform in our ministry.

Do a little teaching reminder, again using Scriptures God has used to convict you, and suggest that the greatest and safest way to be affirmed is in intimacy with God and through humbling yourself before people. You could suggest or assign our book on humility as a project to learn the true secrets of success in the Kingdom of Heaven on earth.

In addition, for those in supervision of ministry staff or volunteers, I highly recommend our course, called Ministry Foundations 101. It is designed to help leaders equip ministry workers with the foundational attitudes and knowledge to work on a ministry team. It was developed after counseling pastors and leaders who were struggling with lack of unity and personality clashes, etc., on their ministry teams.

NOTE: I mention my other books quite frequently in this one. It sure looks like I am trying to sell books and make myself known. I acknowledge that it gives me pleasure when people read my books and get blessed by them. However, I am committed to fighting my pride in this area and making this all about expanding His Kingdom. My books are not "my books." They were inspired by downloads from the Holy Spirit, and I give Him the credit for any insight that blesses someone. I have also found a way to give the books away for free for those who download e-books. Also, in our public meetings, we have all our books available for free.

When Your Humble Appeal Falls on Deaf Ears

There is no guarantee that your appeal will change someone's heart. Some people feel they have too much to lose to acknowledge failure or mistakes. Such were many of the Pharisees and Scribes, etc., in the New Testament. But most leaders should respond favorably, if you can focus on their own potential favor and blessing from God, based on Matthew 6:33, the verse that tells us that natural blessings await those who seek first God's Kingdom and His righteousness.

However, if you are working in a ministry position under the leadership of someone who rejects your appeal, you may have to make some difficult choices. Obviously, you could spend more time praying, which could include fasting. If you are actually employed by the ministry under the leader in question, you will probably have to do more soul searching and seeking the face of God for wisdom. You may have a family to think about and they might need to be a part of any decision.

The other option, which should only be considered after serious searching your own heart and seeking the wisdom from above, would be to graciously resign from that position. This should never be out of hurt feelings, anger, bitterness or revenge. If you are struggling with these, then you need to work on your own manifestations and roots of pride before trying to fix someone else's problem.

If you are in authority over individuals who reject your appeal and you have truly humbled yourself and done all that you can do to make them feel loved and affirmed, you again have to make some difficult decisions. This time, you need to consider their situation as you would your own. If you ask them to withdraw or resign from their position, how will it affect their future and their family? This cannot be the issue that makes the determination, but it should always be a consideration, demonstrating the Father's heart of compassion.

If you give the person time to review his decision, keep on praying that God will show them His love and his or her pride. I would bind the spirit of pride and any other spirit that manifests itself, like insecurity, self-pity and anger. Ultimately, it is their choice, but we can make it as easy as possible for their sake and the sake of the Kingdom of Heaven. After all, Jesus shed His blood for them and longs for them to repent and be restored.

If we do release them from their duties, it should be with sincere grief, knowing that they are hurting and will hurt even more as long as they are not willing to humble themselves. There should be no joy or feeling of power when we send people away from the ministry they have been serving. It should really break our hearts, just like it breaks the Father's heart.

Hopefully, you won't have to either leave a ministry or fire someone from a ministry, but if you do, these guidelines, along with the ever-present voice of the Holy Spirit, should help you to do what needs to be done, in order for you to be faithful to your commitment to always seek first His Kingdom and remain a part of the Kingdom-Building Church.

4. Empower Marketplace Ministers

The next suggestion addresses the need to expand your Kingdom-Building Ministry outside the walls of your church facilities. There are a number of important things that can be done to accomplish a paradigm shift as to what is truly ministry.

to the ministry in business or education or government, etc., as we do who serve as pastors, etc.

This would help people get a vision for themselves of being "in the ministry." They may hate the idea of being on the church stage in the spotlight, and having to perform in front of a crowd. But if they could be recognized as "in the ministry" serving on a different "mountain of society" they would be greatly encouraged, and it would help your ministry transition from a "church-building church" to a "Kingdom-Building Church.

5. Challenge Every Religious Tradition

Every denomination or ministry that has been around for a while will have developed a number of traditions. The longer the ministry has been around, the stronger the traditions will be. In addition, many new movements continued some of the traditions of their former denominations.

For example, we know that Martin Luther became convicted about the doctrine of Salvation by Grace, and when his attempted reforms were rejected by the Catholic Church, he founded the Lutheran denomination. But, although he was persecuted by the Roman Catholics for his non-conformity to the churches traditions, he and his followers were soon persecuting the Anabaptists for believing in and practicing adult baptism after conversion and immersion, rather than sprinkling. He also clung fiercely to the doctrine of transubstantiation, which teaches that the bread taken in communion literally becomes the physical body of Jesus.

It is very difficult to overstate the power of tradition. We assume the way we do church is both normal and biblical, but seldom do we ever challenge what we normally do or how we normally do it.

For example, why are church leaders called "Pastors?" Almost every leadership title has the word "pastor" attached, such as Senior Pastor, Associate Pastor, Seniors Pastor, Children's Pastor, Youth Pastor, Worship Pastor, etc. Yes, there are a few people in position, who are not called pastors, such as board members, elders and deacons, trustees, etc., but those who lead departments are almost all called "pastors."

If you check out the New Testament record, there were actually no church leaders in the book of Acts who were identified with the title, "Pastor." The elders were told to "shepherd the flock" by both Peter and Paul, so we can assume they were the pastors within the congregations, but there were none that were identified as the chief leaders of a city church. They were simply the mature and wise Christians within the church of their city who helped bring spiritual stability among the people. Churches were run by apostles, both senior apostles, like Paul, and junior apostles, like Timothy. As mentioned in a previous chapter, there were other individuals that were called teachers, prophets and evangelists, but no mention by name anywhere in the New Testament of anyone in particular with the title of pastor, other than Jesus, the Good Shepherd.

NOTE: Pastor and Shepherd are the same word in the Greek, as well as every other language I have checked out. Only in English do we have two separate words.

This is just one example of traditions we assume are the normal biblical model. There are many more. Church furniture, times of gatherings, order of service, etc., are all difficult to trace to examples in the New Testament church. And perhaps the most important accepted tradition of all – many different denominations and churches in the same city, which do not often have any fellowship with each other.

Let's look at church furniture. The pulpit and the pew did not originate in the early New Testament church. There is nothing evil about them, but neither is there anything sacred about them. If anything, they perpetuate a dichotomy of the clergy and the laity. Some are professional ministers serving spiritual food, while others are there to be fed and taught and the status of most of them will never change.

Having church services Sunday morning is a well-established, if not sacred tradition. Even the time of the service has been strictly observed by some denominations. When Martin Luther broke away from the Roman Catholic Church, he did away with the early morning mass. Actually, he changed the times of service more than once, moving the time later and later in the morning. The reason he did this was that he loved to party on Saturday night and wanted to sleep in longer. It may seem like I'm picking on poor old Martin Luther, but he is the best known Reformer and a man of great accomplishments, so he is a great personality to use for an illustration.

Most Christian churches have made the exact time for services a flexible option, but the Sunday morning meeting is still pretty much a sacred tradition for most of them. For some folk, it doesn't seem like they've been "to church" if it's not on Sunday morning. I know it's true that Scripture mentions a couple of times that people gathered on Sunday, but we have no biblical instructions to do so.

For some deeper insights into the Sabbath and the Lord's Day, I highly recommend our book called, *Holy How – Holiness, The Sabbath, Communion and Baptism.*

And then there's the order of service, which we're all familiar with. We all know what to expect and in most cases there's a bulletin with the exact order of events which have been carefully planned to fit into the time slot each event is given. Sometimes the exact minute on the schedule is printed out for those on the program. Such highly planned schedules are practical and make for efficient use of time, especially for churches with multiple Sunday morning services, but they don't give much room for spontaneous creativity or a move of the Holy Spirit, such as happened frequently in the book of Acts.

How about the way we train ministers? Were there any seminaries for Paul or Timothy where they could attend, study, earn degrees and get ordained? Did Jesus insist that His disciples go to college before He could make apostles out of them? Obviously, the answer to all the questions above is "NO."

I'm not saying that what we do is wrong, but neither is it necessarily the normal from God's perspective, like it is for us. What we assume is normal is that young people who feel a "call" to ministry, rather than a "secular" career, go to the seminary or Bible college of their own denomination and after graduation, seek a position as a pastor or missionary in that same denomination.

God's Training Corral

God recently gave me a vision and a word of a new wineskin that He is releasing to the new generation of ministers. I saw a large corral where horses where being trained for service. The corral had several strong fence posts. These posts were a play on words. They were not only fence posts, but they were like a military "post." They were individual training centers.

Young horses would be brought in and would be stationed at a particular post, to be trained in the skills of the particular post. When they had completed their training under the mentor at that post, they would be moved to another post. They might spend time at three or four different posts before they were released to serve outside the training corral.

I believe these posts were various mature spiritual mentors or ministry training schools, such as our Kingdom Sending Center that God instructed us to start in Illinois. But God has called us to specialize in certain things and He has called others to specialize in other things. This concept helps to more fully equip disciples of Jesus for their particular calling and destiny. We are one post where people can be trained, but learners can spend time at several other posts to become more fully prepared for the challenges they will face.

How about the way we accept the fact that there are so many different churches in the same city that seldom fellowship at any level with each other? How about the way churches are named, such as "The First _____ Church of _____." Of course, in some cities there may be the Second and the Third church of a particular denomination. Can you think of any reason to call your church "The First Church" other than pride?

Paul harshly criticized the spirit of division in I Corinthians 1, where some said they were of Peter and others of Paul and others of Apollos. Some were "more spiritual" and said they were of Christ. There is no mention, however, of more than one church in any city. Paul did not instruct Titus to ordain elders in every church. He instructed him to ordain elders in every CITY. (Titus 1:5)

I personally believe that the fact that we simply accept the status quo in this regard, without crying out to God to break down the walls of division, is one of the worst sins of the current church. There is absolutely no doubt that God's Kingdom will not grow like He wants it to until the church of the city begins to work together as one church. There may be gatherings in different places in the city, but there is only one church, according to the biblical record.

These examples of accepted traditions that we have mentioned serve to awaken us to the fact that we take so many things for granted, as being normal or "biblical" when they are simply our religious traditions developed for either practical reasons or else imported from other religions that merged with Christianity in the earlier centuries. Most of our traditions have served a purpose and have not been bad or evil in themselves. But if we want to walk in the wisdom of God, by following the voice of His Holy Spirit, it would be a good idea to ask Him if it's time for change or a paradigm shift in these traditions or customs.

6. Don't Expect Sameness - Expect Newness and Creativity

I love the many Scripture passages that talk about "new things" that God will do. In Isaiah, He also talks about new things "springing forth." (Isaiah 42:9, 43:19, 44:3,4) We are also told in some places to forget the things of the past because of the new things that are coming. In Revelation, Jesus declares that He is making all things new. He is creating a New Heaven and a New Earth for us all.

God is a Creator and has made us in His image. If we are in the image of the Creator, my logic tells me that we should also be creators. He made us with incredible gifts of creativity, as evidenced by man's amazing accomplishments in so many fields of science and technology, medicine and agriculture, the fine arts, preforming arts and athletic achievements. I don't believe God wants us to be creative in all those other areas, but never creative in the way we present the gospel or relate to one another in the body of Christ.

In fact, Jesus said that the Kingdom of Heaven was like a scribe who brought out of his treasury things old and new. There is a powerful dynamic released when we are able to connect the old treasures with fresh treasures of revelation and wisdom. I find this one of the most exciting things in my ministry, both when I'm speaking to a group and when I'm writing a book. When I get up to speak or when I sit down to write, I usually have a good idea of what I'm going to communicate, but almost invariably, I get something brand new to go with the older truth. When the old and the new come together, wisdom, knowledge and understanding go to another higher level and life begins to be more fun and to make more sense.

For this to happen, we need to have a hungry heart for more of His direction and power in our lives. Basically, we need more of Him! We need to listen and hear His voice and we need to see His vision for our service and devotion to Him.

Chapter 5

Great News ~ A Shift is Happening

God is doing a powerful thing in our generation. He is awakening the bride of His son to His passion for intimacy with her. He is wooing and romancing her into the depths of His amazing heart. God is sharing His Kingdom-building plans with her and she is becoming infected with the idea of becoming a powerful warrior bride. The result is that major obstacles to the explosive growth of God's Kingdom are being brought down and overcome. One of the biggest of these is the widespread belief among Evangelical Christians in the doctrine of Cessationism.

1. The Cessation of Cessationism

The doctrine called cessationism has a variety of forms. In my book, Catching Up to the Third World, I compare it to the theory of evolution, which also has a variety of forms. The reason I find the two theories similar is because of the powerful motivation to believe them, on the part of their adherents.

Generally stated, cessationists believe that miracles, signs and wonders are not for today. They were only for Bible times, when people didn't have the whole Bible. They also state that the miraculous events were only to introduce the gospel to convince people that God was real. Somehow, they reason that now that we have the Bible, which totally illustrates and confirms the power of the miraculous, we don't need the miraculous anymore. That includes prophetic words, healing the sick, raising the dead, etc. In other words, most of what Jesus told His disciples to do when He sent them out two by two in the gospels, and then again in Acts 1, just before He departed from them, we are not to do anymore. In fact, the very tools He gave them to reach the lost are not available anymore either. Note the following passage from Mark:

"And they went out and preached everywhere, the Lord confirming the word through the accompanying signs. Amen." (Mark 16:20)

The signs were given to confirm the word, just like the signs given to Moses confirmed the word to Aaron and the Children of Israel. If we say Scriptures have replaced signs to confirm the Word, we are saying the Word confirms the Word. That would be like saying, "If you don't believe me, just ask me. I'll confirm that what I said is true." That wouldn't go over so great in a court of law, and it doesn't always impact the unbeliever that well either. However, when the Holy Spirit's anointed Word is confirmed by a supernatural miracle – something they can see with natural eyes – the confirmation is powerful and very convincing, as we can see from many, many biblical examples. I found about 90 such examples in Scripture as I did the research for my book, *Signs and Wonders ~ To Seek or Not to Seek.*

And somehow, cessationists believe that the power of the Holy Spirit, that Jesus promised His disciples when He left (Acts 1:8), was soon to be taken away, as soon as all the New Testament books had been written and the apostles had gone home to Heaven. But when Jesus said, "These signs shall follow those who believe" (Mark 16:17), He didn't say, "until the Bible is finished." When Paul said, "Pursue love and desire spiritual gifts, but especially, that you may prophesy" (I Corinthians 14:1), he didn't say, "until all the apostles are dead." Frankly, I believe the logic behind cessationism is as pathetic as anything we know of in the realm of theology.

Understanding the Motivation of Cessationists

What then makes so many theological leaders adhere to this insanity? I am totally convinced that the reason they accept this doctrine is that when they don't have the miraculous happening, and they feel they are as spiritual as anyone because of their high ecclesiastical position, they must justify their lack of power. Thus, even as the theory of evolution was so quickly embraced by the scientific community without a real shred of evidence, people will believe what they want to believe, so they don't have to change the way they live.

Decades ago, in a university philosophy class, I read an essay by William James, which I never forgot. It was called, *The Will to Believe.* James asserted that the power of the will to believe what you want to believe is often stronger than the power of the mind to think logically to the right conclusion. If you really want to do something, you can convince yourself that it's the right thing to do. I sometimes refer to this tendency as "The Doctrine of Justification by Rationalization."

Religious leaders don't want to face the fact that they have religion without the power of God. Scientists don't want to face the fact that they will have to answer to a Creator when they die. Church leaders don't want to change the way they do church and admit they are spiritually powerless. Scientists don't want to change the way they live, which they would have to do if there is a God they must answer to. They both want to justify themselves rather than admit they need to change their ways.

But the Good News Is:

Cessationism is dying. I call it the cessation of cessationism. The signs are now manifesting of its timely demise. Ultimately, all but a few hardened theologians will be forced to admit they were wrong about God withdrawing His power on purpose. Instead, we will understand that miracles decreased, not because of God's desire, but because of the increase of the spirits of division, pride and religion. But the increase in the manifestations of the Holy Spirit's power and might will totally dismantle the arguments for cessationism. When people need a miracle, like their dying child being healed, and a believing believer releases a miraculous healing into the child's body, they will disregard the belief that miracles don't happen anymore.

Other proofs that cessationism is dying are being manifested in the evangelical world. For instance, the Southern Baptist Missions department recently changed their hard stance against allowing their missionaries to speak in tongues.

In early 2015, a Christianity Today headline read: IN-TERNATIONAL MISSION BOARD DROPS BAN ON SPEAKING IN TONGUES. Under the new IMB's president, David Platt, a new simplified set of rules was adopted for the 4,800 missionaries in the Southern Baptist denomination, which eliminated the ban on speaking in tongues. This is a huge shift and follows a softening stand against spiritual gifts for American pastors as well. The fact that the majority of Southern Baptist pastors voted for David Platt, knowing his beliefs, is a good indication that cessationism is losing its grip on them as well.

Another huge anti-cessationist influence is that of a very prominent pastor and prolific author, named John Piper. A strong Calvinist with a huge following, he is a self-proclaimed "continuationist." He believes that spiritual gifts were intended to continue throughout the church age. He finds no reasonable argument against his stand from those who believe in cessationism.

These are just two of the significant inroads being made into the cessationist camp. I believe there are many others and that there will be many more to come.

So how does the cessation of cessationism relate to the subject of this book - the Kingdom-Building Church? This is a very important question, and I pray that those who read this book will develop the appropriate spiritual passion to change much of the way we do church today.

A Little Church History

Cessationism perpetuated the long-standing traditions of the Dark Ages. Religious activity was ritualized and repeated over and over without any interference from the Holy Spirit.

Although some adjustments were made because of the restoration of truth since the beginnings of the Reformation, new rituals and practices were adopted to replace the old ones. They, at first, brought some new life to the religious services, but the new life soon became institutionalized and ritualized like the previous practices.

But what was needed the most, which was to follow the positive changes in doctrine, was the reintroduction and restoration of the miraculous power of the fruit and gifts of the Holy Spirit. This restored power would propel the proclamation of the restored true gospel into every mission field of the earth and bring about the final harvest so Jesus could return and claim His lovely bride.

But the enemy of Jesus Christ and His body, the church, had a plan to thwart the restoration process. When people began to rediscover the power and gifts of the Holy Spirit, the enemy stirred up the pharisaical spirit in the religious leaders of many denominations and movements. A spirit of jealousy entered their hearts. They needed a weapon to fight the rapidly exploding Pentecostal movement of the early twentieth century.

The doctrine of cessationism was their weapon of choice. Many boldly proclaimed the new movement was of the devil and warned their people to stay away. In spite of this warning, millions of hungry souls left their traditional churches and joined the movement that offered them more than theology and religious traditions and rules.

However, others stayed loyal to their traditional churches, wanting to play it safe and not be involved in "emotional" outbursts or "holy roller" manifestations. Positions hardened and cessationism strengthened its grip on millions of church members.

It's a New Day

Today, with the explosion of information on electronic media, church leaders have a much harder time to keep their people under their ecclesiastical control. At the same time, many church leaders are tired of resisting the very thing their soul longs for and their ministry sorely needs. They see what God is doing for others. They secretly crave more of God and His manifestations. Thus cessationism is losing its strongest advocates and the enemy is losing his ability to restrict the expansion of the Kingdom of Heaven on the earth.

Clearly, when miracles, signs and wonders increase, the church becomes a Kingdom-Building Church. For substantial verification, please read, *Signs and Wonders ~ To Seek or Not to Seek*. With a release of the current passion for intimacy with God, the church is losing its desire to build a memorial to itself or its leaders. Instead, church leaders are saying, "We don't care about our personal popularity. We want to make Jesus famous in the earth. He must increase, and we are willing to decrease for that to happen."

A Prophecy for the Kingdom Harvest ~ Smith Wigglesworth

Meanwhile, while the devil was trying to keep the church in a weakened condition, God, as usual, had a plan to counteract his strategy. Although, the evangelical church hierarchy and their followers were being robbed of the blessings of the power of the Holy Spirit, they instead were focusing their attention on the rest of the Word of God. They studied and taught the Old Testament and New Testament with great diligence and thoroughness, albeit without believing miracles were for today's church. They did, however, became the people of the Word. In fact, some not in their camp have accused them of having a different trinity – Father, Son and Holy Bible. At the same time, those who whole-heartedly embrace the complete work of the Holy Spirit have been accused of neglecting the Word and creating their own theology and doing that which is not biblical.

One of the most unusual miracle ministries of the early twentieth century was that of a British man named Smith Wigglesworth. His methods employed in healing were quite radical, but incredibly effective. God used this man to bring forth a powerful word near the end of his life. Being British he talks about a move in Great Britain, but we know that the moves that affected Great Britain were international moves of God, and certainly applied to North America and the church in general. This word was released to the church in 1947. I copy it below.

Two Distinct Moves

During the next few decades, there will be two distinct moves of the Holy Spirit across the church in Great Britain. The first move will affect every church that will receive it, and will be characterized by a restoration of the baptism and gifts of the Holy Spirit. The second move of the Holy Spirit will result in people leaving historic churches and planting new churches. In the duration of each of these moves, the people who are involved will say, "This is the great revival." But the Lord says, "No, neither is this the great revival, but both are steps towards it."

Word and Spirit

When the new church phase is on the wane, there will be evidenced in the churches something that has not been seen before – a coming together of those with an emphasis on the Word and those with an emphasis on the Spirit.

When the Word and the Spirit come together, there will be the biggest movement of the Holy Spirit that the nation, and indeed the world, has ever seen. It will mark the beginning of a revival that will eclipse anything that has been witnessed within these shores, even the Wesleyan and the Welsh revivals of former years. The outpouring of God's Spirit will flow over from the UK to the mainland of Europe, and from there will begin a missionary move to the ends of the earth.

This, I believe is a very significant word, and one that I believe with all my heart. When the people of the Spirit and the people of the Word both realize they need the other group to be complete, God will honor that humility and pour out His glorious power and might on His beloved church. His church, in return, will pour out their lives as an offering to Him in gratitude for what He has done. They will then pick up their tools and begin, in glorious unity, to build and expand the glorious Kingdom of their Bridegroom King.

A few years ago, I felt led to write my first totally fictional book, which was an allegory of the church, as it related to the spirit of religion as opposed to the presence and power of the Holy Spirit. The book is *Veggie Village and the Great and Dangerous Jungle*. It is not a children's book per se, but it will appeal to the reader with an adventurous heart. It is another very prophetic book, which relates to the rejection of the devilish doctrine of cessationism.

2. The Convergence of Crises and Kingdom Empowerment

In the days ahead, I believe we will begin to see the makings of what is often called "The Perfect Storm." We will see a convergence of a variety of crises and shakings on the earth. You can read much more of my predictions in *The Ultimate Convergence*, which was graciously endorsed by Dr. C. Peter Wagner and others.

NOTE: The things I have predicted and prophesied in the book mentioned above and in the paragraphs below are a combination of my own prophetic insights and the gathering of the words and privileged information from others. Because of multiple confirmations from the Lord, I firmly believe in these predictions and am very excited about the future.

The crises that converge on our political systems and international economies along with major natural disasters, will cause people to lose all faith in their human institutions and people will look for supernatural answers to the many emergency situations that they face.

At the same time, God will have prepared a number of incredible and miraculous interventions and inventions that will reveal both His love and His wisdom. The powerful shaking of all the world's trusted systems will open the hearts of people to God and His Kingdom. Governmental leaders will be toppled overnight and new men and women of God will rise up suddenly to replace them. These new leaders will be those with multiple spiritual gifts such as supernatural wisdom, knowledge and faith.

Out of the ashes of man's worst nightmare will arise a people with a godly dream and a vision for an explosive expansion of

God's Kingdom. Churches who had been focused on building their own little kingdoms will see the potential of pooling their resources with other churches to win their communities. Financial resources from Heaven, through divinely inspired new technology will empower those whose hearts have been purified in the fires and the floods. The storms of life will bring the seeds of future blessings and conquest for Kingdom expansion.

We have many exciting days and years ahead of us, and I don't think things will ever be boring for Christians until Jesus reveals Himself again on His return trip from Heaven. These days will have their challenges, but the days of the greater glory of the latter house (Haggai 2:9) will be worth every challenge.

I had thought this would be the last chapter of this little book, but I didn't have total peace about it. However, I didn't know what more I had to add that wouldn't just be repetition. A few weeks ago, I was given a revelation, which I had shared with my wife and a handful of others. The last time I shared it, Brenda, told me to make sure I didn't forget it. "You need to write it down," she said emphatically.

I assured her that I wouldn't forget it, but over the next twenty-four hours, I felt like God had spoken again to me and showed me that the fresh revelation was the final chapter in my book. So, if you're ready for something that may be a little more controversial, but definitely not old theology, take the risk and read the next chapter.

Chapter 6

The Authority to Forgive Sins

There is a verse in John 20 that I have always kind of avoided. I knew if Jesus said it, it had to be true, but how to understand it was a different story. I felt that those who had tried to practice it had missed it and abused it for their own personal gain and the ability to control people. The problem was that this verse immediately followed a very powerful passage that I did love to preach and teach from.

It wasn't until the past few weeks that I finally felt God had shown me something important for the church to understand, especially if they want to do some serious Kingdom building. So let's look at the verse and the three powerful verses that precede it.

When He had said this, He showed them His hands and His side. Then the disciples were glad when they saw the Lord.

So Jesus said to them again, "Peace to you! As the Father has sent Me, I also send you."

And when He had said this, He breathed on them, and said to them, "Receive the Holy Spirit.
If you forgive the sins of any, they are forgiven them; if you retain the sins of any, they are retained."
(John 20:20-23)

This last verse about forgiving or not forgiving the sins of others is the subject of this chapter, and I believe it is a crucial subject to understand if we truly want to build the Kingdom of our King, Jesus Christ. When we understand the importance of this subject and begin to apply it, the church, which is His body on this earth, will rise up out of its deep sleep and become the force for positive change that God intended it to be.

Let's take a quick look at the key words here: forgive and retain. Strong's Greek dictionary gives the following meanings:

Forgive: The root meaning is "To send forth." It has several applications, including forgive. Basically to forgive here means to send away their sins so they are not attached to them anymore.

Retain: The root meaning here is "to use strength" and is translated as retain, hold fast, keep, etc. Thus Jesus is talking about using the Holy Spirit's power to keep that sin attached to them.

I must admit, as I began to write about this subject I felt very inadequate to really either explain or apply the second part of this verse. I had already experienced the blessings of the forgiving side, but I knew I needed a greater sensitivity to the Holy Spirit to apply the second part. We will see how it was applied by Jesus and the apostles, but our main focus on this chapter, as the title suggest, is on the authority to forgive sins. That, in itself, is controversial enough for me.

TWO IMPORTANT EXAMPLES OF FORGIVENESS

1. Jesus

And when they had come to the place called Calvary, there they crucified Him and the criminals, one on the right hand and the other on the left.

*Then Jesus said, "**Father, forgive them, for they know not what they do**." And they divided His garments and cast lots.*

And the people stood looking on. But even the rulers with them sneered, saying, "He saved others, let Him save Himself if He is the Christ, the chosen of God."

The soldiers also mocked Him, coming and offering Him sour wine, and saying, "If You are the King of the Jews, save Yourself."

And an inscription also was written over Him in letters of Greek, Latin, and Hebrew: THIS IS THE KING OF THE JEWS.

Then one of the criminals who were hanged blasphemed Him saying, "If You are the Christ, save Yourself and us."

But the other, answering, rebuked him, saying, "Do you not even fear God, seeing you are under the same condemnation?

"And we indeed justly, for we receive the due reward of our deeds; but this Man has done nothing wrong."

Then he said to Jesus, "Lord, remember me when You come into Your kingdom."

And Jesus said to him, "Assuredly, I say to you, today you will be with Me in Paradise." (Luke 23:33-43)

Jesus was asking His Father to forgive His tormenters when He was being crucified. As the above story reveals, the torment continued for some time after He asked His Father to forgive them. However, the apparent fruit of His forgiveness comes a few verses later, when the thief recognizes Him as the King of kings. The thief, of course, was not the one for whom Jesus was asking forgiveness, but even though we can't prove that Jesus's prayer for forgiveness for the others influenced the thief's decision, I would bet on it, myself. Someday, in Heaven, I'll ask that man personally, just to be sure.

The important point, however, is that Jesus asked the Father to forgive "them." He may have been asking the Father to forgive all those involved, but even if He was just referring to the Roman soldiers, who were just obeying orders, the same principle applies. He was asking His Father to "send away" their sin of crucifying Him. It's worth remembering that Jesus told Pilate that those who delivered Him to Pilate were guilty of the greater sin.

IMPORTANT NOTE: I personally don't believe Jesus was teaching or practicing total forgiveness of all their sins, (with the exception of the repentant thief) determining their future in Heaven or hell. I believe He was talking about forgiving their particular sins against us when we encounter them. That may become clearer with our next example. Salvation comes only through faith in Jesus Christ, and we cannot give anyone a free ticket to Heaven just by asking the Father to forgive all their sins. They must believe and receive salvation for themselves, like the thief obviously did. Of course, there have been practices in Christianity where people were told they could buy forgiveness for themselves or for their family members. What we are talking about here has nothing to do with such practices.

For They Know Not What They Do

Jesus appealed to His Father for their forgiveness on the basis that they were acting in ignorance, not knowing He was the Son of God. This fact leads me to believe that Jesus was actually not referring to the religious Jewish leaders, when He asked His Father for forgiveness. When He talked with the Pharisees, He said they were guilty, and they were of their father, the devil, because they thought they could see just fine, and were not blind, like the man Jesus had just healed. We will look at this story in more detail a bit later in this chapter.

If we are to apply this principle with the authority Jesus gave to the apostles in John 20:23, we would apply it for the same reason. If we want others to be forgiven for sinning against us, we can use the same reason that Jesus used – they don't know what they're doing.

The Important Question to Ask

It has a rather obvious answer, but for the sake of clarity and application, let me ask this question. Did the Father forgive them or not? If you said, "Yes, of course!" give yourself a pat on the back. How could the Father refuse the Son, Who was giving His life in such a painful death, at the Father's request? Of course, He forgave those men, and their sin against Jesus on that day, was erased from the record books.

Let's now look at the second example, which will give us more insights into this principle of forgiving our tormentors.

2. Stephen

But he (Stephen), being full of the Holy Spirit, gazed into heaven and saw the glory of God, and Jesus standing at the right hand of God,

And said, "Look! I see the heavens opened and the Son of Man standing at the right hand of God!"

Then they cried out with a loud voice, stopped their ears, and ran at him with one accord;

And they cast him out of the city and stoned him. And the witnesses laid down their clothes at the feet of a young man named Saul.

And they stoned Stephen as he was calling on God and saying, "Lord Jesus, receive my spirit."

Then he knelt down and cried out with a loud voice, **"Lord, do not charge them with this sin."** *And when he had said this, he fell asleep. (Acts 7:55-60)*

To File Charges or Not to File Charges

I met a man in Mozambique named Francis, who was commonly called Franci. He was working with Heidi and Rolland Baker of Iris Ministries, and was attacked and killed by some young radicals opposed to their meetings. Franci's body was eventually taken to the morgue, after being pronounced dead by the doctors.

Meanwhile the police captured and jailed one of the guilty young radicals and held him there, waiting for Iris officials to come and press charges. But while the church prayed for his resurrection, Franci came back to life and spoke two words through swollen lips. He said, "Forgive them." Franci was taken back to the hospital and the church with one accord, agreed that they would forgive the murderer.

Heidi and Rolland told the police, "We will not press charges against him – we forgive him." The police were disgusted, and said that was no way to deal with crime or criminals.

Suddenly, back in the hospital, Franci's body was totally healed and the hospital released him. Franci went straight to the police station and asked to see the man who had killed him. He told them (like Jesus had done) that the man didn't know what he was doing. Franci talked to the man and led him to Jesus to have all his sins forgiven. The man went on to Bible School and became a servant of Jesus to his people.

This modern day story is a perfect example of what Stephen prayed to God: "Lord, do not charge them with this sin."

It confirms to my own heart and mind that when we are in a position like Jesus was or like Stephen was, God gives us the authority to ask Him not to file charges against our persecutors. I believe that we have that privilege and when we do so, we give God an opportunity to do a special work in that person's life and perhaps bring them to salvation.

I must now ask the obvious questions again: Did the Father honor the request of Stephen? I'm sure you agree that He did.

One Man Who was Not Charged with Stephen's Murder

We are told by Luke in this account that there was a young man named Saul of Tarsus, approving of the stoning of Stephen. In Acts 9, we read more about Saul's aggressive attacks on the church. With letters of permission from the High Priest in hand, he headed for Damascus to arrest any men or women who followed Jesus. I believe that the prayer of Stephen was instrumental in what happened next to Saul, who of course, became the great Apostle Paul.

As Stephen decided to show mercy to his murderers, so God showed mercy to His young chosen apostolic missionary. In an awesome encounter with God, that left him blind and totally transformed, Jesus spoke to him and in His mercy let him know what he was doing. It was another case of, "Father, forgive him, for he knows not what he's doing."

As we know, the world would never be the same after Saul became Paul and traveled the nations to bring the gospel of the Kingdom to much of the rest of the known world. His letters, or epistles, have been read for two thousand years and have guided the life of the church in so many ways.

Now, perhaps, Saul would still have become the great missionary apostle if Stephen hadn't asked God to forgive him. And perhaps the thief on the cross would have appealed to Jesus without hearing him forgive those who crucified Him. And perhaps Franci would have still been resurrected if Heidi and Rolland hadn't forgiven his murderer. Yes, perhaps! But it seems to defy the odds. I do believe that forgiving those who hurt us, even before they ask for forgiveness, opens them up to the mercy and loving kindness of the Father.

At the same time, if we react in bitterness and a spirit of revenge, we may miss a huge opportunity to empower a vessel that God wants to greatly use in the future. The power of forgiveness is a crucial key to building the Kingdom of Heaven on the earth.

APPLICATION FOR THE KINGDOM-BUILDING CHURCH

So many ministry leaders are hurting because they feel violated by other ministry leaders. Many have accused others of stealing "their" sheep. Church board members have felt the sting of the words of other deacons or elders or even the pastor of their flock. Many have left church after church because of offenses, and pastors have quit the ministry or moved on to another city because people have severely wounded them.

When the above situations happen, they almost always leave both parties, plus many other people on both sides of the battle, in emotional turmoil and badly disillusioned. Churches today are filled with what I call, "wounded warriors." These are Christians who are just holding on to their own spiritual life and salvation. They have little zeal or passion for Jesus and for building His Kingdom.

Some victims of "friendly fire" from other Christians continue to minister but with their defenses built up. They are suspicious of others who might have selfish motives to steal from them and bring them more pain.

For example, a pastor of a large church had a strong prophetic minister speak at his church. The visiting speaker stayed around long enough to draw many of the church members to himself and they left his congregation and started a new congregation. Since that time, that pastor has been suspicious of prophetic people and anyone coming in with a strong ministry. As a result, his church ministry has continued to struggle, although he has a powerful anointing when he preaches and travels internationally.

Another situation taking place is that a youth pastor with several years of service to the youth of his church went off to

Bible College and returned to his city with intentions of starting a new church in the same community. His senior pastor was not happy that he didn't communicate with him about it and feared that the young man would draw people from his church and weaken his own ministry. The great danger is that both parties will be wounded and encumbered by troubled hearts, to the extent that they cannot live the life of freedom and power that God intended them to live.

This kind of unrest among ministers and ministries has done incredible harm to the Kingdom of Heaven on the earth. While God desires that we lay aside our personal ambitions and reputations to help build His Kingdom, too many of His leaders are busy building and defending their own little kingdoms from rival kings.

The tragedy is that most church leaders deeply love God and want to build His Kingdom. They would never think of themselves as being builders of their own kingdoms. And yet, when their ministry is threatened by others, they tend to forget the greater good and get into warfare mode, instead of Kingdom-building mode. They are fighting not their real enemy, but those who should be totally committed to fighting side by side against their common enemy.

THE BETTER RESPONSE

My advice to the senior pastor whose youth pastor planned on starting a new church would be first to ask the Father to forgive him. He really doesn't know what he is doing or how much pain he may be causing. Rejoice that another church will be established to reach people that his church would possibly never reach. This will hopefully help to expand and build the Kingdom. Also thank God that he was given the privilege to mentor and train the young man who will now put to practice what he has been taught.

Finally, I would encourage the senior pastor to take the young man out to dinner and congratulate him on his plans to plant a new church. He could offer to help him get started and encourage him to ask for help. He could invest what resources he could into the young man's ministry and become a valuable spiritual father to him. This would not only be healthy for his own heart and soul, but it would make a huge difference in the future ministry of the young man, who really doesn't know what he is getting into. As one who has planted and pastored a new church, I don't envy the young man the challenges he faces. I feel like Jesus would look down from the cross and say to them, "Young man, behold your father, and father, behold your son."

Forgiving and loving those who hurt us will always be freeing to our own spirit and will often enable those who hurt us to move forward into the purpose and plan of God. Doing what comes naturally for our flesh, on the other hand, will always hurt us and will tend to limit the Kingdom-building potential of our offender as well.

In other words, to be a true Kingdom-building leader or church, we need to deny our own flesh and desire to defend our "territory." It may not be easy, but Jesus never promised us an easy life. He did promise to be with us and reward us and fill us with His joy. A person in ministry with a bitter heart is seldom filled with joy. Those who willingly lay down their own lives and ministries will not only be filled with the Joy of the Lord, but they will become more and more fruitful in their service to the King of kings.

SINS THAT WE RETAIN

As I mentioned earlier, this is a harder subject for me to deal with, but I do feel that it must be addressed. First, we need to look at some Scriptural examples.

1. Jesus

We know that Jesus did retain the sins of the Pharisees who opposed the gospel. Notice this example:

> *And Jesus said, "For judgment I have come into this world, that those who do not see may see, and that those who see may be made blind."*
>
> *Then some of the Pharisees who were with Him heard these words, and said to Him, "Are we blind also?"*
>
> *Jesus said to them, "If you were blind, you would have no sin, but now you say, 'We see.' **Therefore your sin remains**." (John 9:29-31)*

At this point, I believe that what Jesus meant when He said they would have no sin if they were truly blind, was that He could say, "Father, forgive them, for they know not what they do." However, these men had no excuse. They weren't seekers of the truth. They were men filled with pride who wanted to protect their position of prestige and power. They fought Jesus because they felt threatened by Him. Jesus judged them, not because they hated Him, but because they were opposing His Father's will for their own selfish gain.

2. The Apostles

As usual, we find the apostles following in Jesus' footsteps. Both Peter and Paul allowed those who opposed the gospel to receive punishment for their sins.

We have already mentioned the story of Ananias and Sapphira in a previous chapter. They were about to bring the sin of deception for the sake of their egos into the early church. Peter confronted them with a probing question, which they answered with lies. Peter did not show mercy in this case, but allowed their sin to receive immediate punishment. Peter knew by the Holy Spirit that their sin would hinder the expansion of the Kingdom of Heaven on the earth and that God's discipline would bring a reverence and holy fear into the church, which would be used to expand the King's domain on the earth.

Paul, also had some occasions to allow the sins of those who opposed to be punished. Let's pick up the story of Paul and Barnabus ministering to Sergius Paulus, a proconsul, in Paphos, on the Island of Salamis.

> *But Elymas the sorcerer (for so his name is translated) withstood them, seeking to turn the proconsul away from the faith.*
>
> *Then Saul, who also is called Paul, filled with the Holy Spirit, looked intently at him,*
>
> *And said, "O full of all deceit and all fraud, you son of the devil, you enemy of all righteousness, will you not cease perverting the straight ways of the Lord?*
>
> *And now, indeed, the hand of the Lord is upon you, and you shall be blind, not seeing the sun for a time." And*

immediately a dark mist fell on him, and he went around seeking someone to lead him by the hand.

Then the proconsul believed, when he saw what had been done, being astonished at the teaching of the Lord. (Acts 13:8-12)

Once again, we see an apostle, while being full of the Holy Spirit, pronouncing judgment, or discipline, on a man who was serving the devil and opposing God, trying to keep another man from receiving the gospel. If there is ever a time for us as men and women of God to retain the sins of anyone, I believe it must be clear that they are trying to stop the growth of the Kingdom. In addition, we need to be very much under the strong direction of the Holy Spirit.

Some people, including leaders, may say, "Well, I'm Spirit-filled, so I have the authority to speak judgment on those that oppose me."

I would say to them, "Not so fast! Just because you've had an experience in the past with the Holy Spirit, doesn't mean you are always giving Him total control. Check your heart. Are you personally offended, or are you genuinely jealous for God's Kingdom?"

Most of our judgment of others is because we have been personally attacked and want revenge. We defend our own honor and pride much more that we defend the King, like Peter and Paul did.

So please, this practice is mainly for those who have a very mature, and apostolic call. Those who have been much with Jesus and have a proven record of laying down their lives and dying to their flesh. It's not for those who want to prove their spiritual power to others. And, of course, it has to do with specific sins, not whether they are going to Heaven or hell.

THE CALVARY HEART

I felt prompted by the Holy Spirit to relate a story that my mentor shared many times as I traveled in ministry with him. It was one of my favorite messages that he preached in other churches, and it always produced wonderful fruit.

Elmer Burnette had an incredible testimony. His salvation experience thrilled me every time I heard it. After his conversion he discovered he had cancer. Although he didn't believe in healing, God healed him after the doctors had given up on him. Then God gave him an amazing and wonderful healing and deliverance ministry, through which he led thousands to Christ and planted seven churches before he received his reward in Heaven. When I met him I was very impressed with several things about him. First, he really truly loved people with the love of God. It flowed out of his heart like a river. Secondly, he manifested the power of God with many healing miracles. Thirdly, he didn't promote his own ministry like many evangelists, but had a humble heart and never asked for an offering or told anyone but God about his personal needs.

Elmer traveled much around the United States and Canada, mostly as a Christian and Missionary Alliance evangelist. It was a difficult lifestyle, traveling from church to church and leaving his wife and four children behind most of the time. One day, his heart gave out as he ministered at the altar. His doctor told him he was not to preach again until his heart had been rested and restored.

After some time went by he gained some strength and was asked to come preach at an Alliance church in Albuquerque, New Mexico. They needed a pastor and were hoping he could fill the position. The offer was so generous and he needed the income, so he accepted the position without really seeking God about it.

When he and his wife, Evelyn, arrived at the Albuquerque airport, he was taken immediately to a hospital to pray for a lady named Mary, who was giving birth and was in danger of losing her life in the delivery. Mary, by the time they arrived was doing better and Evelyn asked her if she had names for the baby yet. Mary responded that she did not, because she wasn't sure who the father was. Elmer said that a lot of foul language followed that remark.

Elmer, who was not used to a stable income or a steady home life with his family, gave himself energetically to helping the church recover from some difficult times and situations. He and Evelyn went daily to visit Mary and to pray with her. She seemed to be making progress and they were encouraged with her spiritual growth.

After about one month of this, Elmer happened to be on the side of town where Mary lived. His wife was still at home and Elmer thought that just this once he could make a quick pastoral call on Mary, rather than crossing town to get his wife first. When he knocked at her door, Mary's greeting caught him completely off guard.

"I'm so glad to see you came alone, today. I've been waiting for this moment."

I don't remember what else she said, but Elmer was horrified and then became angry. I remember his response very well.

Elmer said, "Mary, after all these times we've come to visit you, you would do this to me. You would ruin my marriage and my ministry."

She responded, "Oh, it wouldn't ruin your ministry."

Then Elmer said the following whenever he shared this story: I don't know if I said it out loud, but I at least said it to myself and God heard it – "Mary, I'm done with you. We've come to visit you for a whole month and if that's the way you're going to respond, then as far as I'm concerned, you can just go to hell."

Elmer shared his experience with his elders and told them that he was done with Mary. His elders agreed that he had done far more than was expected of him and that he could stop going to her home for prayer and Bible study.

Soon, Elmer's heart began to give him major problems again. The doctors wanted him to stay in the hospital but he refused. Instead, he was allowed to go rest in a cabin on a mountain side near the city. The church continued to pay his salary, but he had no resources to pay for a long hospital stay. In the cabin he would have access to a nurse in an emergency by pulling on a string connected to a neighboring cabin. After sixty-two days of total confinement, Elmer had one of the most powerful and impacting experiences of his life.

Suddenly, he became aware of an unusual presence in his room. Then he heard a voice saying, "You don't love my people." Elmer was shocked and convinced that this was the voice of the enemy.

"I rebuke you, in Jesus name. The doctor says I'm sick because I loved God's people too much."

But the presence wouldn't leave and he heard the voice again. He rebuked it again, but to no avail. Finally, convinced it might be God, he cried out. Who don't I love, Lord?"

"You don't love Mary!" came the answer. "You are asking me to heal you because you have a bad physical heart. Mary has a bad spiritual heart and you said she could just go to hell."

"But Lord, you know what she did to me. She would have ruined my marriage and my ministry. I went to her house every day for a month. I can't love Mary."

"Your problem is that you don't have a Calvary heart."

"What's a Calvary heart?"

Elmer always said at this point. "Don't ask God a question unless you expect an answer." He relates that immediately he was in a trance-like vision of Calvary. Jesus was hanging on the cross and he could see and hear the drops of blood hitting the ground. He saw the soldiers gambling over his clothing. Then he heard Jesus utter those powerful words, "Father forgive them, for they know not what they do."

Elmer wept like a baby, but responded back to God, "But that was you, Lord. You are the Son of God. I'm just a man. How am I supposed to love like that?"

Elmer goes on to tell what happened next:

Immediately, I was seeing Stephen, the martyr, being stoned to death. I saw stones flying through the air like sand, there were so many. As he knelt down, he cried out, "Lord, lay not this sin to their charge."

That was as much as Elmer could take. He wept and begged the Lord, "Please let me go back and pray for Mary. I don't care if you ever heal me. I just want to see Mary saved."

All night Elmer prayed for God to bring Mary back to Himself and for the opportunity to minister to her one more time before he died.

The next day, Evelyn came up the mountain in a borrowed

white station wagon, with a bed made up in the back. The doctors wanted to do some more tests on his heart and she was coming to pick him up. He was overjoyed to see her.

Elmer told Evelyn that he was so happy he was going home because he needed to call Mary. Evelyn, a wonderful woman of God that we and everyone else loved dearly, scolded Elmer, saying, "If you're going to start ministering again, I'm not taking you back to town. Promise me you won't call Mary."

Elmer said, "Okay." to calm her down, but knew that somehow, God was going to give him the chance to help her find God. They arrived at their home planning on going to the heart clinic the next day.

About 3 AM, the phone rang beside his bed. He picked up the phone and heard deep sobbing. He said, "Hello, this is Elmer."

The voice, said, "Oh, I'm so sorry. I didn't know you were home. I would never have called you. I just need somebody to tell me how to get back to God."

In the next few moments, Elmer led Mary in a prayer of repentance and the healing of her broken heart. The next morning, Mary brought other family members to receive the salvation of their souls. It was a glorious morning. But he still had to keep his doctor's appointment.

Suddenly, Elmer felt something happening in his body. He told Evelyn, "Something is happening in me – either I'm going to die – no I'm not going to die. I'm being healed."

Evelyn whisked him off to the heart clinic where some of the best cardio-vascular doctors in the nation served a multitude of patients. The first thing they did was to send him for X-rays. The doctors were confused. There must be something wrong with the X-ray machine. They sent him to a different floor with a different X-ray machine. Again, they found no problem with his heart. Finally, frustrated, they sent him to another clinic across town. The doctor there, not knowing Elmer's history, said, "It looks like you may have had a problem in the past, but your heart is perfect now.

While Elmer was sick and in total confinement for sixty-two days, he had promised God that if He healed him, he would go back into evangelism, even if the closest place was more than five hundred miles from home. After being healed, Elmer resigned from his church, to the deep consternation of his board. They had paid his salary while he was sick and now that he was well, he was leaving them. He explained that he had to obey God.

Without telling anyone else, including his District Superintendent, or any other pastors, he went home to a telephone that was ringing off the hook. Calls were coming from pastors all afternoon until he had several months of meetings booked and the closest church was over five hundred miles from home.

About a year later, Elmer was invited back to speak as an evangelist to the church in Albuquerque. Before the Sunday morning service began, he asked the new pastor, "How is Mary doing?"

The pastor said, "Just look. Here she comes pushing someone in a wheelchair. Mary is the biggest soul winner this church has ever had."

Elmer would always remind us at this point in the story, "And I had said, she can go to hell."

ASKING OURSELVES THE TOUGH, PROBING QUESTIONS

» Do we have a Calvary heart that loves like Jesus and Stephen?
» Would Mary have become a soul winner if Elmer had not forgiven her and asked God for a Calvary heart?
» Are there people who are not fulfilling their Kingdom-building potential because we have not forgiven them?
» Do we do what Jesus told His disciples to do?

"But I say to you, love your enemies, bless those who curse you, do good to those who hate you, and pray for those who spitefully use you and persecute you,

That you may be the sons of your Father in heaven; for He makes His sun rise on the evil and on the good, and sends rain on the just and the unjust.

For if you love those who love you, what reward have you? Do not even the tax collectors do the same?" (Matthew 5:44-46)

There are a few other questions we should ask at this point:

» Am I doing everything I can to break down walls with other churches and leaders?
» Is there a way I can invest in other ministries where I have nothing to gain?
» Am I willing to lose all my people and my ministry if it would help build the Kingdom?

GET EXCITED

If we exchange our own means of self-preservation (our pride) for God's hand of blessing on our lives – in other words – if we seek first His Kingdom and purpose with all our hearts to build it, regardless of what people think of us, then every good and perfect gift that the world seeks after will be added onto the amazing benefits God has already given us – forgiveness of sins, a mansion in Heaven and the never-ending glorious presence of the Living God, our Father, our Creator, and our Best Friend.

Amen!

About Ben Peters

BEN R. PETERS has been a student of the Word since he could read it for himself. He has a heritage of grandparents and parents who lived by faith and taught him the value of faith. That faith has produced many miracle answers to prayer in their family life. Ben and Brenda have founded a ministry in northern Illinois called Kingdom Sending Center.

They also travel extensively world-wide, teaching and ministering prophetically to thousands annually. Their books are available on most ereaders and all other normal book outlets, as well as their website: *www.kingdomsendingcenter.org*

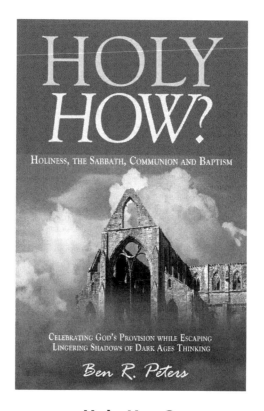

Holy How?
Holiness, the Sabbath, Communion and Baptism
by Ben R. Peters

Available from Kingdom Sending Center
www.kingdomsendingcenter.org

A Mandate to Laugh
Overcoming the Sennacherib Spirit
by Ben R. Peters

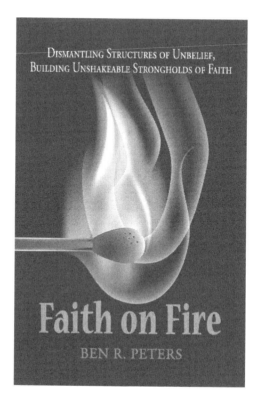

Faith on Fire
Dismantling Structures of Unbelief,
Building Unshakeable Strongholds of Faith
by Ben R. Peters

Available from Kingdom Sending Center
www.kingdomsendingcenter.org

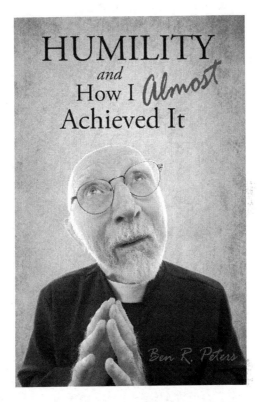

Humility and How I *Almost* Achieved It
Uncovering a Highly Valued Key
to Lasting Success and Kingom Power
by Ben R. Peters

Available from Kingdom Sending Center
www.kingdomsendingcenter.org

The Boaz Blessing
Releasing the Power of This Ancient Blessing
Into Your World Today
by Ben R. Peters

Available from Kingdom Sending Center
www.kingdomsendingcenter.org

"The Ultimate Convergence is imminent and I am excited with all that God is going to do." ~ Dr. C. Peter Wagner

BEN R. PETERS

The Ultimate Convergence
An End Times Prophecy of the Greatest
Shock and Awe Display Ever to Hit Planet Earth
by Ben R. Peters

Available from Kingdom Sending Center
www.kingdomsendingcenter.org

**Veggie Village and the Great
and Dangerous Jungle**
An Allegory
by Ben R. Peters

Available from Kingdom Sending Center
www.kingdomsendingcenter.org

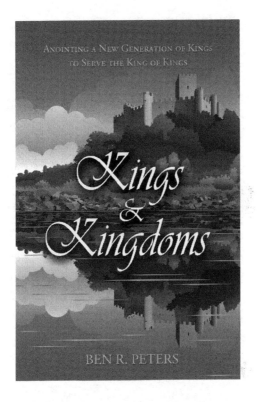

Kings and Kingdoms
Anointing a New Generation of Kings
to Serve the King of Kings
by Ben R. Peters

Available from Kingdom Sending Center
www.kingdomsendingcenter.org

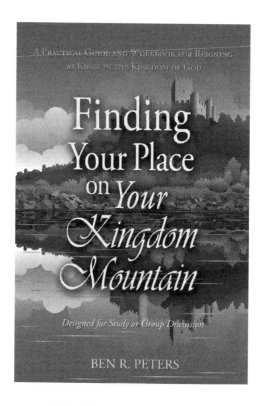

**Finding Your Place
on Your Kingdom Mountain**
A Practical Guide and Workbook for Reigning
as Kings in the Kingdom of God
by Ben R. Peters

Designed for Study or Group Discussion

Available from Kingdom Sending Center
www.kingdomsendingcenter.org

Catching up to the Third World
Seven Indispensable Keys
To EXPLOSIVE Revival
in the Western Church
by Ben R. Peters

Available from Kingdom Sending Center
www.kingdomsendingcenter.org

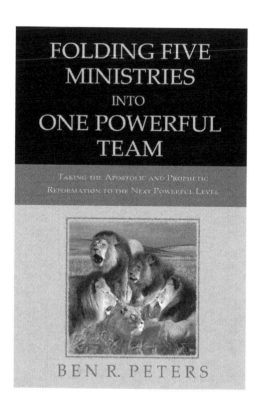

Folding Five Ministries Into
One Powerful Team
Taking the Apostolic and Prophetic Reformation
to the Next Powerful Level
by Ben R. Peters

Available from Kingdom Sending Center
www.kingdomsendingcenter.org

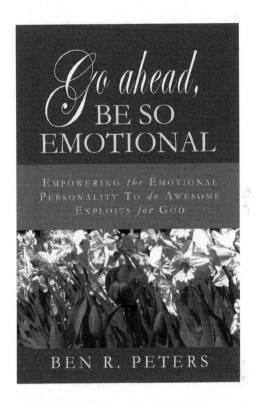

Go Ahead, Be So Emotional
Empowering the Emotional Personality
to do Awesome Exploits for God
by Ben R. Peters

Available from Kingdom Sending Center
www.kingdomsendingcenter.org

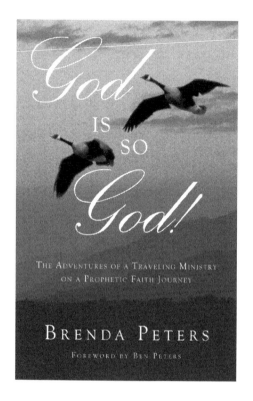

God Is So God!
The Adventures of a Traveling Ministry
on a Prophetic Faith Journey
by Brenda Peters

Available from Kingdom Sending Center
www.kingdomsendingcenter.org

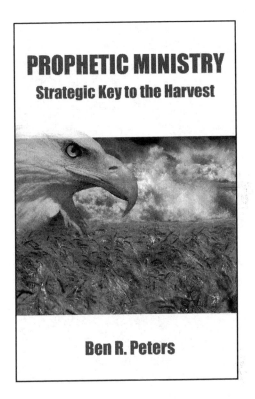

PROPHETIC MINISTRY
Strategic Key to the Harvest

Ben R. Peters

Prophetic Ministry
Strategic Key to the Harvest
by Ben R. Peters

Available from Kingdom Sending Center
www.kingdomsendingcenter.org

Resurrection!
A Manual for Raising the Dead
by Ben R. Peters

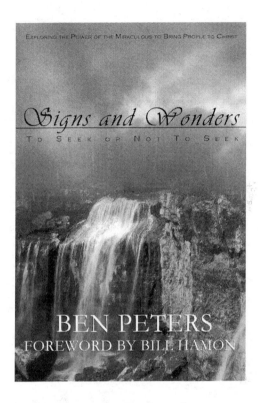

EXPLORING THE POWER OF THE MIRACULOUS TO BRING PEOPLE TO CHRIST

Signs and Wonders

TO SEEK OR NOT TO SEEK

BEN PETERS
FOREWORD BY BILL HAMON

Signs and Wonders
To Seek or Not to Seek
by Ben R. Peters

Available from Kingdom Sending Center
www.kingdomsendingcenter.org

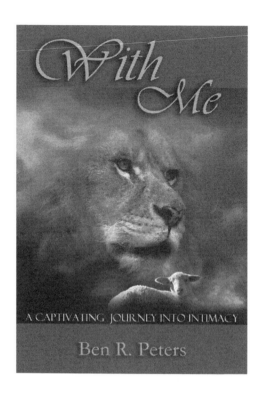

With Me
A Captivating Journey Into Intimacy
by Ben R. Peters

Available from Kingdom Sending Center
www.kingdomsendingcenter.org

Holy Passion: Desire on Fire
Igniting the Torch of Godly Passion
by Ben R. Peters

Available from Kingdom Sending Center
www.kingdomsendingcenter.org

Birthing the Book Within You
Inspiration and Practical Help
to Produce Your Own Book
by Ben R. Peters

Available from Kingdom Sending Center
www.kingdomsendingcenter.org

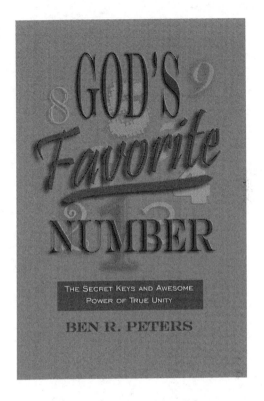

God's Favorite Number
The Secret Keys and Awesome
Power of True Unity
by Ben R. Peters

Available from Kingdom Sending Center
www.kingdomsendingcenter.org

Made in the USA
Columbia, SC
10 September 2017